HAUNTED
DORCHESTER

HAUNTED DORCHESTER

JULIE HARWOOD

First published 2008
Reprinted 2020

The History Press Ltd
97 St George's Place, Cheltenham,
Gloucestershire, GL50 3QB
www.thehistorypress.co.uk

© Julie Harwood, 2008

The right of Julie Harwood to be identified as the Author
of this work has been asserted in accordance with the
Copyrights, Designs and Patents Act 1988.

All rights reserved. No part of this book may be reprinted
or reproduced or utilised in any form or by any electronic,
mechanical or other means, now known or hereafter invented,
including photocopying and recording, or in any information
storage or retrieval system, without the permission in writing
from the Publishers.
British Library Cataloguing in Publication Data.
A catalogue record for this book is available from the British Library.

ISBN 978 0 7524 4816 9

Typesetting and origination by The History Press Ltd.
Printed in Great Britain by TJ International Ltd Padstow, Cornwall.

Contents

	Acknowledgements	7
	Bibliography	9
	Introduction	11
one	Dorchester – The Town	15
two	Dorchester – Suburbs and Surrounding Areas	67

Acknowledgements

I would like to thank the following people for their help and contributions:

Southern Paranormal UK, especially the members of the Dorset and Hampshire team who have investigated some of the documented locations; my good friends Jazz Bettany and Simon and Rachel Steadman, who are a constant support in helping me with my research; the Thomas Hardy Society in Dorchester; Sue Randall of Weymouth, Lisa and Ralph Pwenzikia of Dorchester; Claire Stevens of Romford; Kevin Jones and family from Dorchester; Mary Windsor and Sue Wilson from Poundbury; Brian M. from Dorchester; the Tolpuddle Martyrs Museum; Rachel Gibbs, Kingston Maurwood Animal Park, Gardens and College; Jed Briggs and family.

Thanks to the many others that have helped me with this book including my boyfriend Tony, my family and work colleagues at Livability who have allowed me annual leave, often at short notice, to jet off to Dorchester to follow up on a report; and of course all my friends.

All photographs are copyright of the author.

Dorchester beer mats welcome people to the town.

BIBLIOGRAPHY

Books:

Douet, James *British Barracks 1600-1914*
Ellis, Chris and Owens, Andy *Haunted Dorset* (2004) SB Publications
Martine, Arthur *Martine's Handbook of Etiquette and Guide to true Politeness* 1866
Matthews, Rupert *Haunted Places of Dorset* (2006) Countryside Books
Miles, Dorinda *Hutchins History of Dorset* (1870)

Websites:

www.localhistories.org/Dorchester – Tim Lambert's Dorchester
Lawrence of Arabia – the Imperial War Museum London website – www.iwm.org.uk
www.visit-dorchester.co.uk
www.wikipedia.org – the online encyclopaedia

Introduction

Dorchester lies on the south-west coast of England in the county of Dorset. A popular holiday resort close to Weymouth and Lyme Regis, Dorchester it is also the largest town in west Dorset. The town's history can be traced back 4,000 years when the Celtic Durotriges tribe farmed the land, their main settlement in Dorset being Maiden Castle. Dorchester, or Roman Durnovaria, 'the place with fist-sized pebbles', was first recorded in the the fourth century in the *Antonini Itinerarium*, a register of stations and distances along roads of the Roman Empire. Durnovaria was, at this time, a main market town and one of the chief settlements of the remaining Durotriges. The Romans built a wall around the town, an eight-mile aqueduct to supply the town with water, and converted Maumbury Rings (a Neolithic henge) into an amphitheatre. The stone walls, however, were built as defence as the Roman civilisation was in serious decline due to the fierce Saxon raids on the east coast of Britain. Little is recorded in the sub-Roman period, although it is thought that the town was abandoned after the Roman withdrawal.

By 864 Durnovaria and its surrounding land was dominated by the Saxon Dorsaetas. They renamed Durnovaria as 'Dornwaraceaster', or 'Dornwaracester', and over the years the name changed further until it became known as Dorchester and thrived as a political and commercial centre for south Dorset.

In 1610 a charter was presented to the town which reformed its local government and gave the residents certain rights (this was followed up by another charter in 1630 highlighting further reforms). Fires ravaged the town in 1613, almost completely destroying the town.

Soon to become part of Dorchester's new development, Brewery Square, this old building would have employed many local people.

By 1642 the Civil War had broken out in England, and Dorchester, being predominantly Puritan, supported Parliament. Even though the town was fortified it was captured by the Royalists in August 1643. Although the Royalist soldiers moved on they returned to the town in 1644, but were defeated by the Puritans.

During the 1700s Dorchester suffered another four fires resulting in a ban on thatched roofs in 1776; the ban is still in force in the town centre today.

During the sixteenth and seventeenth centuries, Dorchester's wool industry thrived; however, by the eighteenth century it had almost completely died, being replaced by a successful brewing industry.

In 1685 a rebellion in the south-west led by the Protestant illegitimate son of Charles II, the Duke of Monmouth, was thwarted, first at Bath in Somerset and then Bristol. James II had been warned of Monmouth's plans and the Royal Navy captured Monmouth's ships, giving him no way of escaping to Europe. He was eventually captured and beheaded for treason. This led to the infamous court cases led by Judge Jeffreys,

The notorious Judge Jeffreys' lodgings, Dorchester.

named the 'bloody assizes', where Monmouth's supporters were put on trial. They were executed, and their heads were impaled on spikes and displayed as a warning to others.

Dorchester saw many improvements over the following years, including the introduction of gas lighting in 1835, and the opening of the county hospital in 1841.

In 1840, Thomas Hardy was born in Higher Brockhampton, just outside Dorchester, and the poet William Barnes also lived in Dorchester from 1837 until 1886.

In 1848, a corn exchange was built in the town which provided a place for trading grain. In the 1850s sewers were dug and by 1860 the town had piped water.

Although Dorchester has continued to grow, it is still a relatively small-sized town. The brewing industry thrives, and advances in technology have brought related industries into the area.

With its rich history I wondered if this may be one of the country's most haunted towns. I know there are plenty of stories to be told about apparent hauntings in and around the area, but do these relate directly to Dorchester's history or are they merely stories and legends passed down over the years? I have recorded many of the accounts I have been told or that I have heard about, although I cannot personally vouch for the truth behind these tales. The purpose of the book is not to prove or disprove the paranormal or the existence of ghosts. Instead, it is to disclose a little local history with each story and tell the fascinating tales of haunted Dorchester and let you, the reader, decide for yourself.

one

Dorchester – The Town

The Town Pump Bucket Boy

The old town pump, located on South Street close to the old corn exchange and the stunning clock tower, is considered to be a central point in Dorchester. It appears to be a perfect place to begin relating strange sightings in Dorchester. Today it is an obelisk to mark the old pump's location, and it plays an important part in Dorchester's tourist industry, being a central meeting point for groups visiting the town. Dorchester is one of the few towns in the country still to have their own town crier and it is by the pump that he makes his announcements. Alistair Chisholm is the current crier and Britain's Town Crying Champion. He is also a registered Blue Badge guide, conducting tours around some of the town's most well-known and historic buildings.

The original Roman pump supplied the area's water and was a vital part of Durnovarian life. It was a great feat for its time, pumping water from the nearby aqueduct. The area around the pump is now pedestrianised, but in Roman times the area would have been far busier, being the heart of the settlement and a main trading area. Even though the system was not sanitised, it was unequalled by any other system in the country until the nineteenth century. The original water pump was two very simple pumps joined together with a piston on each side. These were raised and lowered by a handle which sucked water through a one-way valve, and subsequently out in a jet into the awaiting containers. With the history

Will you spot the ghost of the little boy near Dorchester's town pump?

of the pump in mind, it is easy to assume that any spirit appearing by the pump would be related to the Romano-British period.

A small, bare-footed ghost of a child wearing dirty clothing has been observed by the pump. Few people have reported seeing his face as most of the sightings have been from behind. He is observed for a few seconds as he leans towards the pump and holds a wooden bucket-like container. Obviously no water is seen coming from the landmark (real or spectral). However, when he seems to have finished collecting, he stands up straight and simply disappears. The most fascinating aspect about this sighting is that the boy is observed in broad daylight and these kinds of sightings are getting rarer over the years. He is seen as clearly as though he is real, and the only reason people question what they have seen is because of what he is wearing (though many people believed at the time they were watching some kind of modern day re-enactment) and that he disappears after people have watched him for a short time.

Locals believe that his spirit is referred to as a stone-tape recording – a ghostly image from the past recorded in the fabric of an area and, as the name suggests, this can be especially prominent if stone has been used in construction, as it is widely believed to hold energy and memories. The boy never makes any attempt to interact with people, and never looks anywhere other than at the pump. He is always sighted at roughly the same of time of the day, and always for the same amount of time, seemingly completing the same task over and over again. All this ties in very well with the stone-tape theory that the locals believe, and you will certainly hear it mentioned again in this book when people refer to other haunting tales in the town.

Durnovaria Town Walk

The Durnovaria Town Walk is a circular trail around Dorchester and gives an insight into its Roman occupation, in particular as to how the town was defended under Roman rule. The walk can take from one to two hours, and is well worth the effort. It is along this walk that strange lights and sounds have been heard by walkers. They have been experienced around the remains of the old Roman wall where a plaque has been made from part of its remains. It was donated to Dorchester and its mayor by Lucia Catharine Stone, a local woman who wanted to donate something to her home town that would be preserved. It is certainly eye-catching and it is also around this area that reports have been made of bright lights floating through the air and the sound of marching has been heard.

Part of the Roman walk around the outskirts of the town.

One couple reported that, after a Christmas shopping trip, they decided to do the walk by twilight before they went home. By the time the couple reached the remains it was starting to get dark and they commented that they should have bought a torch. Despite it being dark, the couple remember it was not bitterly cold – that was until they started to pass the remains. They then appear to have been subject to a cold blast of icy air that made them feel as though they were stepping into a walk-in freezer. However, they quickly seemed to walk out of the other side. Neither of them could understand what was happening, and as they passed out of the ice-cold spot they took two steps back to try and relocate the spot. It was so cold that the lady actually started to shiver, but the air temperature suddenly returned to normal. It is well known that cold and hot spots are commonly linked to spirit presence; is it feasible that these cold spots could be an indication of a spirit or is it simply just fluctuating air temperatures depending upon the conditions at the time? Was the area protected or were they near water?

I took all this into consideration until the couple described what happened next. As they stood there chatting about the strange temperature change they had experienced, they both heard the sound of marching

Part of Dorchester's Roman wall.

which gradually faded away. As they stared in disbelief they realised the marching sound was getting louder again, as though it was coming towards them. Then, seconds later, the footsteps appeared to be right in front of them together with the icy-cold blast of air. As quickly as it had come, the cold breeze disappeared.

Not really sure what to make of this, the couple headed back the way they had come and sadly never completed the walk. They felt as though someone was patrolling the area and that they were in the way. As the marching was experienced by the old Roman walls, could this have been the spirit of Roman soldiers guarding the perimeter of the town?

Any good paranormal investigator, once they have heard a claim of a paranormal experience, begins research to find out whether there is any other report from the area or building to corroborate the sighting. Although I investigated, I could find no other report of marching. I did, however, speak to a lady who just happened to be passing the wall and she said she had seen what she described as spectral lights. These are little flashes and dots of light (often white or green in colour), that can be seen by the naked eye and cannot be explained by normal occurrences such as passing cars, street lights, reflections and so on. She first saw them out of the corner of her eye and when she turned to look at them closer, they seemed to be travelling with her as she walked along the path. They appeared at shoulder height, and she described them as being similar to a beam from a miniature torch or laser pointer. She admits that she was not scared as she was sure they would have a normal explanation, but, as she continued walking, she noticed that they started to go back the way they had come. After about ten seconds, they stopped briefly, (but did not disappear) and then started coming back towards her. Making the most of her headstart, she continued on her way. After a couple of minutes they were gone.

The lady did not report her experience initially, but decided to come forward when I placed an advertisement asking for accounts of anything strange people may have experienced in Dorchester. This occurrence or possible paranormal sighting could have just been forgotten, but instead it has helped substantiate other people's experiences in the area. Is this the spirit of a Roman soldier who is keen on making his protecting presence known to people that pass by?

The Ghost Writer

A large, regal-looking statue stands proudly in Colliton Walk. Sculpted by Eric Kennington, it was erected in 1931 and is dedicated to Dorchester's most famous literary son, Thomas Hardy.

Hardy was born in Higher Bockhampton near Dorchester on 2 June 1840. At the age of sixteen he helped his father, a master mason and builder, with architectural drawings for a restoration project at Woodsford Castle. The owner, architect James Hicks, was so impressed with young Hardy's work that he offered him an apprenticeship with his firm in Dorchester. Hardy trained fervently, and in 1862 moved to the bright lights of the capital to work for prominent architect Arthur Blomfield. He also enrolled at Kings College London, where he won awards from the Royal Institute of British Architects (RIBA) and the Architectural Association. While in London, he also wrote a number of poems; however, despite his success in the world of architecture, his poems were constantly rejected by the publishers he approached. It is believed that although Hardy enjoyed life in London, he never truly felt at home, and when his health started to deteriorate, he returned to his home town at the age of twenty-one.

In 1870 Hardy met Emma Lavina Gifford, his future wife, when he went to work in Cornwall to plan the restoration of St Juliot's Parish Church. For years he continued to write, and although his first novel,

Antelope Walk, Dorchester, now home to many local businesses ... and ghosts.

The Poor Man and the Lady, was completed in 1867, he failed to find a publisher. His literary mentor, fellow novelist and close friend George Meredith, urged him to continue. In 1871, *Desperate Remedies* was anonymously published, followed by *Under the Greenwood Tree* in 1872. The first novel published under his own name was *A Pair of Blue Eyes* in 1873, which documented his courtship with Emma. In late 1874, he was able to complete one of his most important novels, *Far from the Madding Crowd*, and its success allowed Hardy to give up his architectural work and concentrate on his first love – literature. Over the following twenty-five years, he published a further ten novels, although these years were not always filled with joy. The couple became estranged, but when Emma died in 1912, Hardy was devastated. He returned many times to Cornwall and to places they visited, and in the poems he wrote over these years (1912-1913) his grief is evident.

In 1914 Hardy married his secretary, Florence. However, their marriage was tarred by his preoccupation with Emma's sudden death. He tried to deal with this by continuing to write poetry, and works such as *Satires of Circumstance* (1914), and *Moment of Vision* (1917), were published when Hardy was at his lowest emotional ebb.

In December 1927 he became seriously ill with pleurisy and died in January 1928. His final poem was dedicated to his first wife Emma, whilst he was on his death bed. Ironically, it was dictated by Hardy to his then wife, Florence. His funeral took place at Westminster Abbey and there was much debate about where he should be buried. Family and friends wished him to be buried with his mother, Jemima, in Stinsford, Dorchester, yet the executor of his estate, Sir Sydney Cockerell, was adamant he was buried in the Poet's Corner at Westminster Abbey. After a bitter argument, a compromise was reached between the two parties, and it was decided that his heart would be returned home to Dorchester, while his ashes were to go to the Poet's Corner. Shortly after his death, all his letters and notebooks were burned by the executors.

On Colliton Walk, not only can you see a statue of Hardy looking down over the town he loved, it is said on some nights you may also see the apparition of this literary genius. Late at night, visitors are often greeted by the sight of a smartly dressed gentleman with dark hair and a twisted, greying moustache. Despite his well-presented appearance, he is reported as looking sad and lost. He slowly paces back and forth in front of the statue before stopping still, looking around, and then gradually disappears into the cold night air. I mention cold night air, as sightings of this apparition are mainly confined to the month of January. One gentleman reported that it was too dark to see the statue on the night that he saw the apparition, so he revisited the spot in the daytime and then realised it was Thomas Hardy he had seen. Is this the restless spirit of Dorchester's very own Thomas Hardy or is it another spirit pacing the town? The descriptions reported are strangely similar to the way Hardy looked in the latter years of his life, and his apparent unrest and sad demeanour relate to his state of mind at the time of his death. Is this sad ghost still mourning the loss of his first wife, or is he indeed left in limbo due to the way he was buried? It would certainly be interesting to know if this spirit has also been seen in Westminster Abbey where his ashes are buried – there may then be an answer to some of the questions raised by this paranormal sighting.

The Teddy Bear House

What better way is there to attract spirit children than a museum full of antique toys and teddy bears? An Edwardian house, converted from a coaching inn located in Antelope Walk, is home to Mr Edward Bear and his family of people-sized bears! From antiques to modern-day items it is a haven for children of all ages, and it is here, in one of the ground floor rooms, that Sue told me about what she saw one summer afternoon in 2007.

She had taken her four young granddaughters on a day out to Dorchester and on their list of places to visit was the Teddy Bear House. They were aged between four and eight-years-old, and as they were admiring the displays in the lounge room with the white lady bear and the boy bear, Sue noticed a sudden coldness even though it was a very warm, muggy day. She did not think anything of it apart from the fact that it was very refreshing, until she turned around to speak to one of the children. Behind her granddaughter stood another little girl of a similar age and build but she was very pale and Sue described her as 'not quite solid, like a hazy reflection in a pond'. As Sue stood transfixed on the little girl, the child just smiled at her and walked away. Sue rushed after her but she was nowhere to be seen. Sue is very positive about what she saw and, although the girl was ashen, she believed she was happy and certainly felt nothing untoward in the house, even after the sighting. She believes that the child spirit was attracted to the house not only because of the teddy bears but also because of the large amount of child energy. There is certainly a theory of attracting 'like for like' in a paranormal context, although this is not shared by everyone in the paranormal investigation and research field. The historical period of this child is hard to place as Sue admits she was mostly obscured by her granddaughter. Sue is certainly not scared of the house and continues to return there in the hope she may see her again one day.

The Phantom Sobbing Lady

The Dorset County Museum was founded in 1846 to help protect and record Dorchester's rich heritage and natural environment, located in one of the town's prettiest buildings, a gothic-style building dating back to 1884. It is, without doubt, one of the best places to visit if you want to find out about Dorchester and the surrounding area, and has on display a

The Dorset County Museum where phantoms have been seen.

wide range of items, from fossilised dinosaur footprints to original Thomas Hardy manuscripts. The Victorian Hall is the main gallery in the museum and is breathtaking in itself. Built in 1883, it was inspired by the Great Exhibition of 1851. The cast-ironwork arches and stunning rose window is a magnificent backdrop to displays ranging from Tudor paintings to contemporary work by sculptor Alan Marsh (1912-1997). The floor of the hall has Roman tiles and mosaics inlaid into it. These were taken from excavations of Roman town houses from in and around Dorchester. The hall is also used for an exciting range of performing events and has been described as having some of the best acoustics in the south of England.

So could a mixture of good acoustics and old Roman flooring support some possible paranormal reports in the hall or could it help to explain them? The two people involved have very different opinions on this. One lady I spoke to, who would prefer to remain anonymous, is sure that a building containing such an eclectic array of items would be haunted. She strongly believes in the stone-tape theory of hauntings and, because some of the items are so old, they contain energy and 'recordings' of times and possible people gone by. Even though she is not a direct employee of the museum, she has spent many hours there, often late into the evening, and has experienced first-hand what she describes as the sobbing lady. Whilst alone in the hall one evening, thinking about a project she was working on, she was interrupted from her train of thought by a loud, sobbing noise. She was quite sure she was on her own and was startled by this sudden noise she had not heard before. She was aware of the creaks and moans of the old building, and this was a sound she had never heard before. After a couple of seconds it stopped and so she took one final look around and carried on with her planning. Minutes later, she heard the noise again and this time she really felt as though someone was there with her. Even though the sobbing noise she could hear was fairly loud, she could not work out where it was coming from. As she looked around the sound appeared to move with her and after a while it seemed to be all around her. She was adamant that it sounded like a lady sobbing as the pitch was too high for that of a gentleman, but as the apparent sobbing continued and she could still not see anything, she started to feel uneasy and decided to pack up her kit and leave the area. On the way out of the building she spoke to one of the museum's staff, a gentleman who also spent a lot of time there, and she confided in him what she had experienced. He was very quick to laugh the experience off as a trick of the ear caused by the acoustics of the hall, and informed her that many odd things were often heard.

The lady involved, however, has never been convinced of this explanation. Having worked in many old buildings in her career, she had never experienced anything like it before. So who is right? Is it simply a trick caused by the acoustics of an old building or could this be a paranormal occurrence, a replayed recording of times gone by, coming from the artefacts in the museum, experienced by many people but passed off because of the structure they are heard in? We may never know. However, the people on the two sides of this argument will probably never be swayed, unless of course the sobbing lady of the museum one day decides to show herself!

Members of the Dorchester Volunteer Aid Detachment in 1892.

Dummy Display

When Max Gate House, Thomas Hardy's former home just outside Dorchester, was put up for auction with local firm H.Y. Dukes & Sons on 16 February 1938, the only items that escaped the sale were the pieces of furniture from his study. These items were placed in the care of the Dorset County Museum. Among these were the table and the chair that Hardy worked at when writing classics such as *The Mayor of Casterbridge* and *Tess of the d'Urbervilles*, and various bookcases and cabinets. Along with the furniture the museum was also given many of Hardy's own first editions and the reference books he used while writing his novels. Approximately 400 books were given for safe keeping, as well as many other smaller items such as desk trinkets. The museum set up a display area where they painstakingly recreated the study as it was in Max Gate, so that visitors to the museum could observe Hardy's belongings in as realistic settings as possible. It is in this area that the apparition of a gentleman has been seen sitting in the chair at Hardy's desk. The figure was seen by a local gentleman and a trainee spiritual medium who visited the museum a couple of years ago. As he stood observing the mock up he observed what he believed to be a dummy sitting in the study. He remembers thinking how well the museum had done to get a dummy that looked so like Hardy to go in the display. The figure was motionless and sat facing the desk. The gentleman continued his visit around the museum and decided, just before he left, to return to the study area. He immediately noticed that the dummy had been removed from the display, and after taking a couple of pictures, made his way out of the museum. On his way out he approached a member of staff and asked why the dummy had been removed from the Hardy study display. To his amazement, the woman told him there was never a dummy in the display to remove. Without realising, did this gentleman see the spirit of Hardy? Of all the places Hardy is said to haunt, for me this would be one of the most likely places. Hardy never felt more at home than when he spent time in his study doing what he did best. There are many stories worldwide of items of furniture and objects being haunted by their owners after they have passed away, especially items that the owner was linked to in a special way. There is a belief that if you purchase or own furniture that is not brand new, you are buying furniture with a history that contains energy of its former owner, a past that sometimes items are unwilling or unable to relinquish. Believe it or not, haunted furniture or belongings are highly sort after and there are currently hundreds of internet sites worldwide that claim to be able to sell you haunted items from amulets, often necklaces with a spirit presence to help ward off evil or ghosts with negative intent. Whether you believe in haunted furniture or not, the gentleman that claims to have seen Hardy sticks to his story. Hardy may not have a reason to haunt the museum but he would certainly have an undeniable connection to his own study, so whether this apparent ghost is in visitation or his energy is held in the furniture is unknown. If you ever visit the museum keep an eye out, as you may not only be observing this amazing gentleman's belongings but possibly their owner too!

A Right Royal Haunting

Nestled in the heart of the town on High West Street is the Wessex Royale Hotel. Built in the Georgian period in 1756, it was modelled on a similar design in Bath's Royal Crescent by John Wood. The minute you walk through the door you are treated to true Georgian splendour, with its classical grand staircase, panelling and fireplaces in nearly every room. There is a truly overwhelming feeling of stepping back in time. It is very easy to see why it is such a popular hotel with holidaymakers and business people alike. It is also apparent that some former guests or residents are happy to stay there indefinitely. The following reports are based on stories that have been told to me by ex-staff and former guests.

The first account is of an angry-looking gentleman standing by the open fireplace in the lounge. He has been seen by two people at the same time, which in itself is a rare occurrence, but what is even more spectacular is that he apparently spoke to them. These two ex-hotel employees were cleaning with their backs to the fireplace. Suddenly both reported hearing a male voice say, 'he murdered me here', and both jumped as they had not heard anyone enter the area. They swung round and could see the faint image of a tall, thick-set gentleman standing by the fireplace. He was scruffily dressed in leather, wearing an apron and it appeared that he had been working. He had dark hair and was tanned in the face and both the ladies felt that he was a foreigner, but obviously, from what they heard, he could speak English well. His face looked angry and he was scowling at the women. They also reported an overwhelming smell of beer which had not previously been there. They continued to stare at him in disbelief and then as he started to fade they ran out of the area. Both ladies were shaking – what had they seen and heard? The message that the women heard was clear enough, and suggested that the gentleman had been murdered close by the fireplace, but who was he? He may have been a previous owner of the hotel, and his clothing was of that of the last century. Although no murder has been recorded in that building, not all crimes are documented. An interesting fact is that several people have been reported to have died in the hotel from 'natural causes'. Could this angry spirit be returning to the scene of his murder to let people know that he was killed and did not, in fact, die naturally as could have been reported?

The second report from the hotel concerns a young, professional couple who were staying at the hotel for a long weekend, and it was on the last night that the wife experienced what she describes as 'one of the scariest encounters of her life'. They had an early night as they had to be up early the next morning to travel home, and both had had a busy day and were tired. They had been in bed for about an hour and the gentleman was fast asleep. Claire had just finished reading the last page of her book and had turned the night light off, ready to settle down. As she did she saw a flash of light out of the corner of her eye. She turned in the direction of the flash and turned the lamp back on but there was nothing there. She had a little chuckle to herself as she had watched a few episodes of a popular paranormal investigation show on television, and she knew that they always reported seeing things out of the corner of their eyes. She also knew that experts said that this was nothing unusual, and just eyes catching sight of objects in the peripheral vision but unable to focus on them immediately. Claire knew she was tired and so thought nothing of it, turned the light back off and settled back down. Before she could even close her eyes, she heard a loud bang and saw her book slide off the bedside cabinet. Startled and a little shocked, she turned the lamp back on and leant down to pick the book up. She knew she had not knocked it as she was nowhere near the cabinet and she knew the floor was not uneven as her glass of water was still in place next to where the book had been, and there was not even a ripple in the glass. A little perturbed, she replaced the book on the cabinet, and turned the lamp off for a third time. No sooner had she done this there was a loud knock at the door. Without thinking she jumped up and ran to open it. The knock was so sudden and loud she wondered if there was a problem, but no one was on the other side. A little annoyed she returned to bed only to find that all of the covers were pulled back including her side of the sheet, revealing the bare mattress. Her husband slept on, undisturbed. She remade the bed and settled down to try and get some sleep. As she looked towards the end of the bed she saw a large, swaying, black shape. Pulling the blankets up over her head, she remained there for at least ten minutes. When she ventured out of the covers, the shape had disappeared and eventually she was able to get some sleep.

What was happening in this guests' room that night? Something seemed desperate to draw her attention. It seems sad that there may be a spirit world out there that tries to get our attention for whatever reason, but in fact scares the majority of us. Claire admits that she would love to have known why the things happened to her that night, but in some ways is glad that nothing else happened, as she would have ended up screaming the hotel down. Despite all this the couple still stay at the hotel when they come to visit their family in Dorchester, and Claire insists that people should not be scared about staying there. She suggests for the fainter hearted – if your book falls on the floor during the night, ignore it and leave it there until morning.

Ghostly Hardye

If you see many buildings and statues dedicated to Thomas Hardye you could be forgiven for thinking that the dedications were referring to the

Borough Gardens – the home of a distressed and bloody spirit.

novelist and poet, Thomas Hardy. However, Hardye is a strong local name and many other notable Hardy's and Hardye's in Dorchester's history have been acknowledged over the years, including Admiral Hardy, a local businessman. The Thomas Hardye public house in Dorchester is named after the least-known Hardye, the local merchant and businessman, who in the 1500s ploughed money into the town to raise its status and provide for its residents. He founded the Hardye Foundation, which is most notable for building Dorchester's first free school, or 'Freeschole', in 1569. Today, it is a voluntary-aided school, still supported by the foundation. Despite Hardye's charitable acts, he was also known locally as a part-time pirate. Has his spirit given the inn its name? Situated on Alington Lane, some visitors to the pub have reported unexplained cold spots in certain parts of the bar and unexplainable moving shadows have been observed. Although a welcoming pub, there is an uneasy feel in the cold spots. As far as I am aware from my research, there have never been any unusual sightings at the pub. However, who is to say that the strange face in the crowd on a Saturday night is not Thomas Hardye himself, checking out the bar like any pirate worth his weight in rum would? After all, this is the kind of place he would have felt quite at home!

The Grisly Howler

The Borough Gardens lie minutes from the centre of Dorchester. This beautiful area contains two tennis courts, bowling green, children's play area, bandstand and clock tower, all nestled between stunning flower beds and evergreens. On a warm summer's day it is difficult to find a space in this wonderful area. On a dark winter's night the gardens take on a different dimension, and if you choose to wander through them, then you should be aware of what you may encounter. The gardens were laid out and opened in 1895 and they proved as popular then as they are now. The apparent apparition that has been sighted in the gardens does not appear to have anything to do with the gardens. This is a tranquil place, yet this spirit does not appear to people as being very peaceful. It makes you wonder what was situated here prior to the gardens. The apparition has been seen by a handful of people that have been in the gardens after dark, and they have reported the apparition in the same way despite it being very unlikely that they have ever met or spoken to each other. Everyone reports it as having been a traumatic experience. The woman appears as though she is running towards them, and has been sighted in different parts of the gardens but always presents herself the same way. She is wearing a long, white gown and is bare-footed when she appears. She has long, dark hair which seems dirty and tangled. There appear to be blood stains on her white gown and her hands seem to be dripping with blood in the dim light of the moon. She always stops running before she reaches the witnesses and then she lets out a blood-curdling scream seconds before she disappears. Initially it appears that she has been hurt or is the spirit of a murder victim, although none of the reports document that she is holding herself as though she has been shot, stabbed or injured. Was she murdered or are people in fact witnessing the spirit of a murderess? There is no way to tell. One thing is for sure – if you go walking in the gardens at night, be prepared for an encounter with the Grisly Howler.

Mad at the Makeover

Dorchester has many old inns, and it is above one of these that a local couple were tormented for six months before they could no longer bear it and moved from the property. The couple wishes to remain anonymous, and so for the sake of this story I will refer to them as James and Sarah. The couple had been married before but they met each other shortly after both their partners passed away in the late nineties. They decided not to marry immediately, and as they both worked in the town they rented a small, two-bedroomed flat above one of the well-known local pubs. They would also rather we kept the location of the flat unknown, as there are still tenants renting the flat to this day. When the couple first moved in, the flat was homely but dated, and so they sought the landlord's permission to redecorate it. The landlord seemed pleased with their suggestion and even gave the couple some DIY vouchers in order to buy the paint. They spent weeks peeling off the old, gaudy, seventies-style wallpaper, replacing it with serene blues and greens. They then ripped up the old smelly carpet which ran through the entire flat. Underneath they found a beautiful wooden floor and were tempted to restore it; however, funds were tight so they carpeted throughout. They tried to find some parts of the wood that could be kept bare but unfortunately it was all badly scratched and in need of varnishing so it was impossible. The decorating took James and Sarah approximately two weeks and it was not long after this that they both started noticing that the flat felt very different. The rooms were cleaner and lighter and on the surface it looked homely but what was once a warm flat now felt cold and unwelcoming. The couple would sometimes have the central heating on around the clock in an attempt to warm the rooms up, but nothing seemed to work and they found themselves having to put on extra layers of clothing to keep warm. They would sit and watch television some evenings and could physically feel icy chills blow across their faces and arms even when they knew no windows were open. Things got so bad that on three separate occasions in four weeks they called the gas engineer out, as they were sure something was wrong with their boiler. All the engineer could report was that everything seemed to be working correctly. The couple had to admit that something odd was going on, when one morning they were so cold when they got up that they had to go and sit on towels on the radiator. The radiators were on full but the rooms were just not heating up.

Things started to get more sinister when their personal items, such as hairbrushes, bottles of shampoo, a wallet and so on, started to go missing for days at a time before turning up in the most bizarre places. On one occasion James found his wallet in the refrigerator and Sarah found her hair straighteners in the empty bath. The couple were logical and tried desperately to find sensible explanations for the movement of the items, but in vain. Sarah also started to feel uneasy in the flat, especially when she had to spend time there on her own when James was on a late shift. She felt as though she was being permanently watched even when she was obviously on her own in the bathroom. Her friends even commented that the flat was cold and used to make jokes about it when they came round that they had to put on their winter woollies! This went on for months and soon the couple had to discuss whether they wanted to renew the lease. Sarah was adamant that she wanted to move, but, although James realised that the conditions they were living in were not ideal, the flat was close to the town, their jobs, family and friends. While they were discussing this there was an almighty crashing noise from the kitchen, and both shot up from the sofa and ran to see what the noise was. Sarah likened the noise to someone dropping a pile of crockery on the floor but when they got to the kitchen they could find nothing out of place. They knew a noise could have come from the pub downstairs – after all it was a busy Saturday night – but both reported the sound definitely coming from inside the flat. They returned to the lounge a little confused but continued to discuss the possibility of staying in the flat for another six months. It was an affordable property as far as flats in the town went, and it made good financial sense for the couple; however, it was Sarah's peace of mind that concerned James. Once a fun-loving, outgoing person she appeared to have retreated into herself and was constantly nervous and jumpy. The couple continued to talk until another noise broke their conversation. James and Sarah looked at each other as they listened to the sound of heavy footsteps on wood. Both knew that there was no wood and yet the footsteps sounded as though they were making their way along the hallway to the lounge door. As the noise reached the doorway there was another loud crash; this time they knew exactly what made the noise, and they saw several books fly out of the bookcase as though being swiped by unseen hands. This was enough for the couple and they grabbed their coats and headed straight out of the front door. They stayed that night at a friend's house, and on Monday James made the polite call to the landlord to let him know they would not be renewing the lease. Shortly after they arranged to move out, but Sarah stayed in their new property, unable even to revisit the flat to collect belongings. When James met with the landlord to hand back the keys, he could not quite believe what he heard. The landlord commented that tenants did not stay long; a previous tenant, an elderly woman called Elisa-May Jones, had lived in the flat for almost thirty years before passing away after falling in the hallway. Her family had apparently spent many years trying to get her to move as a first-floor flat

The keep where the lonely soldier still marches.

was not suitable, but she was a stubborn woman and vowed she would never leave. On many occasions the landlord had approached her about redecorating the flat. However, she refused this as well, even refusing to open the door to the decorators when they arrived at the property. So has Elisa May kept her promise? Is she still in the flat guarding her home and was she showing her displeasure when the flat was eventually decorated? Sarah and James believe so, and now they know the story they feel they have a sense of understanding surrounding the strange occurrences in their former home. They believe it must have been very hard for Elisa to see them ripping down her wallpaper and changing the home she obviously loved. All this being said, Sarah's vows she will never go back into the flat and wonders, every time she passes it, whether the new tenants are now the ones being terrorised by Elisa. Thank you to James and Sarah for telling me their story but also to the family of Elisa-May Jones who kindly gave permission for this account to be written.

High East Street, Dorchester, 1900.

Lonely Soldier at the Keep

The Keep Military Museum is a striking landmark that stands on Bridport Road in Dorchester. It was built to resemble a stunning Norman castle and is white in appearance due to the local Portland stone from which it was constructed. It was completed in 1879. In *British Barracks 1600-1914* by James Douet, the Keep is described: 'the "Keep" or armoury at Dorchester was an unusually realistic interpretation of a medieval castle, by the army's standards, which must have been in response to local sensibilities over the historic character of the town'.

The Keep was originally the gatehouse for the Depot Barracks of the Dorsetshire Regiment as well as the County Armoury. The Depot Barracks were the administrative centre for the Dorsetshire Regiment and its centre for recruitment and training. The Keep maintained this function between 1879 and 1958. The only time it was interrupted was during the Second World War, when the barracks were used to house the 701st Ordnance Light Maintenance Company and the 1st Quartermaster of the American Armed Forces. It is this period of time that seems to have left the Keep with its one and only resident phantom, a lonely ghost believed to be the spirit of an American soldier. Footsteps have been heard on the upper floors of the building and a sense of melancholy and loneliness has been felt by people who enter certain areas of the Keep. Although this sad soul has never been seen, icy-cold breezes and the sound of his pacing boots and heavy sighs have been reported by some employees. An ex-employee, and practising spiritual medium, who worked there in the 1980s first picked up on the spirit. He could immediately feel the heaviness and sadness in the air and it did not take him long to realise that it was a male spirit in an American services uniform. He tried on many occasions to make contact with the spirit (when his colleagues were not around) but sadly he could not get the soldier to respond. Why he is there is not known. Does he return there to visit a place where he once served? Is he looking for something or is he attached in some way to some of the items exhibited by the museum? The ex-employee has returned as a visitor several times since he ceased working at the Keep and, even though he could still feel his energy, when he spoke to staff they did not report experiencing any odd occurrences. It is sad – the soldier's story may never be told, and he seems to remain there in silence. Maybe one day he will decide to tell his story, or if he finds what he is looking for, then maybe he can move on. If you visit the Keep, listen for the footsteps of the lonely soldier and maybe just say 'hello' if you feel that cold breeze pass by you.

The High East Street Pincher

On a pleasant day in Dorchester the streets are bustling with a mix of locals and holiday makers enjoying the town. By the time it starts to get dark and the streets are quiet, the Dorchester pincher is known to strike. No one knows where he will be but he likes the ladies. He has only ever been seen by a couple of people, although many have felt his pinch over the years. He is described as a bearded, scruffy-looking man in his late fifties who wears a long, brown overcoat. This cheeky chap is believed to be the ghost of a vagrant called Harry who lived in the town many years ago. He was a well-known figure and there was much local sadness when he passed away from pneumonia in the winter of 1929. Harry meant no harm to anyone but several residents of Dorchester (now in their eighties) remember him from when they were children. One resident remembers his mother and grandmother falling victim to Harry's roaming hand and how embarrassed they were when pinched on the bottom by this rascal. One resident quoted his mother: 'It could have been a lot worse – he could have robbed us and taken our ham'. No one knows why Harry still pinches, but I suspect that after his passing he has decided to return to the place he loved.

The Phantom Pub and the Mystery Motorcyclist

Worldwide ghostly manifestations, haunting ethereal sounds and strange aromas are reported; however, the most bizarre reports are when people recall seeing buildings that are not actually there, and such occurrences test the stone-tape theory to its limit. These interesting and genuine recollections are very rare, yet when more than one person has reported the same phenomena it is difficult not to give the reports credence.

This was the case in Dorchester. Part of the town centre, Cornhill, has been pedestrianised and made a great difference to the area, although several buildings had to be pulled down to make way for the car-free area. One of those buildings was the Antelope public house, which is not to be confused with the Antelope Hotel which formed part of the Antelope Walk. This ageing local public house was demolished to make way for the new area and it was only a few weeks later that the first sighting of the pub took place. A local lady, whose husband was part of the demolition team that brought the old pub to the ground, was walking past the site. She was surprised to see the pub still standing, but put it to the back of her mind as she knew it could not be long before its time was up. She continued on her way home not thinking anything more about it. During dinner, her husband mentioned something that reminded her of the Antelope and she asked him when it was due to be knocked down. She was amazed when he told her it had been done. At first she was positive he was just joking but then she realised he was serious. He explained that the pub had been demolished two days earlier and he was on the team responsible for the job. She explained what she had seen, and her husband could not help but take it seriously.

The next day he spoke to a couple of his colleagues and when he returned that night he was quick to relay his workmates' comments. Apparently the pub was a local haunt for one of Dorset's famous

The spirits of the Old Antelope Hotel still haunt Cornhill.

Cornhill is now a vehicle-free zone.

residents, T.E. Lawrence, the famous Lawrence of Arabia. He was one of the enigmatic figures of the twentieth century and, when he died in 1935, it was a shock to the world. Lawrence lived in a small cottage at Clouds Hill, not far from Dorchester. On 13 May 1935, as he was riding his Brough Superior Motorcycle to Bovington Camp to post a parcel, he had a tragic accident. He suffered severe head injuries and never regained consciousness. He died on 19 May 1935 aged just forty-six. Whilst Lawrence was known to be a quiet gentleman, some considered him a bit of a recluse, who liked nothing more than riding his motorcycle and frequenting a range of public houses. Apparently the Antelope was one of these and it is said that, after he died, a phantom motorcycle had been spotted in front of the old fireplace alongside the grey figure of a rider who was believed to be Lawrence's ghost.

The lady of our story was fascinated when she heard about the sighting and enquired whether anyone else had seen anything strange at the building site. It did not take long for her to find a gentleman who had witnessed the ghostly figure of a gentleman carrying a motorcycle helmet who was standing in the building area. The figure appeared to be staring at the area where the Antelope used to be. Was this T.E. Lawrence looking for his local pub or could it be that the spirit of Lawrence could see the pub as it was, even though it was no longer there, and was blissfully unaware that anything had changed? I think we have to hope for the latter. After a couple of months the site looked completely different, and where the pub had been were now shops. Interestingly, the shop that now stands on the site of the Antelope is also home to strange goings-on. The shelf displays are sometimes rearranged during the night and items have disappeared for no particular reason. Perhaps a building can be demolished but the energy from past beings remains.

The Murderous Reflection

In many horror films and scary movies we see heroes and heroines (and indeed victims) caught unaware by the 'baddie' standing behind them. Only at the last minute are they able to catch sight of the assailant in a mirror or window, and by then it is often too late. Fortunately, this is not usually the case in real life, but the scare of seeing someone behind you, who you did not know was there, is something that frightens many people after watching such a film. Some people refuse to look out of windows when it is dark and often pass mirrors by, worried by the thought of seeing something eerie. One day, a lady called Mary Windsor, was browsing in a small shop in Dorchester's pedestrianised town centre. The shop, which prefers to remain nameless, was decorated a number of years ago with some large, gold, gilt-framed Victorian mirrors (though most of these have now been removed since the shop's refit in 2006).

One winter's afternoon, Mary and her friends were browsing in a quaint little shop in Dorchester. She decided to have a look at some figurines and made her way to the rear of the shop. Behind the shelf that held the figurines Mary noticed a large, beautiful mirror, and she made a quiet comment that it would look wonderful in her lounge at home. After a little convincing from her two friends, she decided to purchase the mirror and, as the sales assistant wrapped it, she informed Mary and her friends that the mirror had come from a large Victorian house in London that was once owned by some very wealthy businessmen. Apparently they had collected 100 mirrors and luckily had a house large enough to display them.

Mary took her mirror home and decided to hang it directly above her fireplace. The mirror made it feel so much larger as it reflected the light coming through the window. She positioned it perfectly so that when she stood in front of the fireplace she could see directly into it. Not long after, Mary found herself regularly using the mirror. She used it to check her make up before leaving for work, and in the evening she would stand in front of it and brush her hair.

One blustery winter's evening at around 10.30 p.m., about a month after Mary bought the mirror, she was brushing her hair in front of it. As she placed the brush down on the mantelpiece she saw a black shape rush behind her in the glass. It moved so fast, it made her jump, and instinctively she swung round, thinking someone had walked behind her. No one was in the room and the house doors were locked. She felt a little nervous as she made her way to bed. However, by the next morning she had almost forgotten about the scare the night before and hurriedly got ready for work. That evening she returned home and began to get ready to go to a party at a friend's house. As she did her make up, her facial expression changed as she saw a gentleman standing behind her in the mirror. He looked sad, and had his hand on his head as though in pain; there was also blood on his face. She swung around to have a better look at him but there was no one there. When she looked back into the mirror a different gentleman appeared, evil looking with dark eyes. She swung round again confused by what she saw; surely someone must be in the house? She sat down, shaking uncontrollably.

A seventeenth-century-style street sign painted on the wall of a building in High West Street.

Mary does not remember much else, only that she went to the party and stayed there the night. She told close friends about her experiences, recalling the story the sales assistant had related. Is it possible that the two men Mary had seen were the original owners of the mirror? Mary and her friend, Sue, decided that they would return to the shop where she had bought the mirror and try and find out if the sales assistant knew anything else about the mirror's prior owners. Luckily the same girl was in the shop and, a little gingerly, they approached her; Mary was rather embarrassed about telling people what she had seen, especially strangers. The sales assistant's reply took them aback – she did not know much about the mirror except that it had been sold because the owners had been killed in a robbery that had gone wrong and the contents of the house were sent for auction. On disturbing the thieves, both men had been hit over the head with heavy, blunt objects, and were killed almost instantly. The sales assistant apologised for not saying anything when Mary purchased the mirror, but did not want to frighten her. Was it the murderer and one of his victims that Mary had seen in the mirror? Amazed and stunned, Mary went straight home with Sue and took the mirror down; she would never feel comfortable with it in the house.

The Balti Express in Icen Way where an inconsolable girl may be seen.

As Mary sold the mirror not long after she took it down, I was unable to see it. However both she and Sue were sensible people who have nothing to gain from telling their story, so I have no reason to disbelieve what Mary saw. Some people do believe that energies and circumstances can be recorded in mirrors; could it be that the energy of the victim and his murderer are indeed captured in this mirror for eternity?

The Distraught Girl

Dorchester has its fair share of takeaway restaurants that cater for many different tastes. The popular Balti Express stands on the corner of High West Street and Icen Way, and both its customers and passers-by have spotted a young, distressed woman who stands under the Icen Way street sign. She is reported as being barefooted, dressed in blue and that the colour of her dress reflects her mood. She leans back against the wall, crying uncontrollably and looking down towards the ground. When she is approached, she continues to look downwards, ignoring whoever may be trying to help her. Frustrated at her lack of response, people have then walked away, but if they look back, she has gone. Some people believe that what they have witnessed is the spirit of a street girl.

One night a woman was waiting by the road, whilst her boyfriend went to a nearby takeaway, when she saw the girl suddenly appear as if from nowhere. She started to cry, and when the woman took a step towards her she completely disappeared

It could be the case that hundreds of people have seen this girl and have not paid much attention to her, thinking she was someone who had been out for the night and was a little 'worse for wear' from drink. In fact, what they could be witnessing is the spirit of a girl who obviously has not moved on, and has to return to the corner of the street until she can be given the help she needs.

The Ghost of Little Tommy

All Saints Road leads off Icen Way and it is here that a local resident, whilst walking her dog, witnessed the ghost of a small boy, aged around five years old, and dressed in Victorian clothing with mid-length trousers, braces and a white shirt. Her first impression was that he was wearing fancy dress and on his way to a party; however, when the woman looked again she could not see anyone with him and he certainly looked too young to be out on his own. She called to the child but he did not react, and so she decided to carry on walking as she would be back in five minutes and decided that, if he was still there, she would call the police. As she wandered away, she glanced back, and amazingly the boy was gone.

The next day she mentioned the young child to a friend, and was surprised by her response. Apparently he has been seen many times and is affectionately referred to as Tommy. He is always seen in the same place and wearing the same outfit. Is Tommy lost as the lady suspected or is he just returning to where he lived many years ago?

Unrest in the Old Crown Court

West Dorset County Council offices are situated on High West Street, and part of the building was once the Old Crown Court. Strange occurrences have been experienced not only by members of the public on tours of the cells and court room, but also by employees. Until Southern Paranormal UK (SP UK) investigated the building in 2006, no sightings had been officially documented. However, after our visit people felt more comfortable to come forward and tell of their own experiences. Built in 1797, this Grade I Listed building was designed by Thomas Hardwick, a London architect, and is famous for the trial of the Tolpuddle Martyrs. They were sentenced to be transported to Australia for swearing an illegal oath and their subsequent involvement in the trade union movement of 1834.

The courtroom appears today as it did at the time of their trial. The Old Crown Court is also the first court in England to have had a press box, which played an important role in spreading the news of trials and sentences. The notorious Judge Jeffreys held court here, sentencing many local men to death by hanging.

With so much history, often of a gruesome nature, it is not surprising that spirits may still live on in the Old Court and cells.

When SP UK visited in 2006, we experienced some strange phenomena – what were they? Could it have been the spirits of the six Tolpuddle Martyrs? Or could it just be the recordings of the many prisoners that have passed through the building over the years?

Tolpuddle is a village just outside of Dorchester and in 1833 it became the centre of trade union activity when the Friendly Society of Agricultural Labourers was established by local gentleman, George Loveless and five fellow farm labourers. Lord Melbourne was Prime Minister at this time and he was against the trade union movement, so when these six men were arrested in 1834 for swearing an illegal oath to the union, and were arrested and sentenced to seven years' transportation to Australia, he did not see fit to oppose the sentence. At the trial the judge and jury were hostile; however, after the men were sentenced there was a massive public uproar throughout the country, and so the men were transported to Australia without delay. Incensed at this, 250,000 people signed a petition, while a procession of 30,000 marched to Whitehall. The sentences were then remitted and the men were given free passage home from Australia. A couple returned to Britain while the majority felt betrayed by their own country, and emigrated to Canada to start new lives.

During SP UK's investigation of the Old Crown Court, unexplained cold draughts were felt including cold spots in the jury box and witness box. The cold spots did not move and, even though it was an old building, the team could not find any explanation for these cold breezes and spots. In the places expected to be colder (i.e. by the door down to the cells), it was in fact warmer. There was much creaking in the room even when the

Now home to West Dorset Council, the Old Courts where Tolpuddle Martyrs saw their fate.

team were still; this was put down to the building settling, but it became unnerving when the creaking started to sound like footsteps coming from the viewing gallery. One of the most intimidating occurrences was when five members of the team heard a long breathing sound behind them, accompanied by the sound of footsteps. It was then that a couple of the team felt on the verge of tears whilst they were in the dock, facing where the judge would have been sitting. Could it be that they were picking up on the emotion felt by prisoners facing the judge's verdict? Several of the team felt they were given the name James and spectral lights were witnessed in the courtroom. The most overwhelming experience was the sense of being watched – so many of these experiences are the same as those experienced by members of the public, such as cold spots and breezes in similar places, the sense of being watched and the eerie sound of footsteps. Down in the cells members of the group sat alone for periods of time. Although the cells were small, they felt as though there were others sitting with them. Heavy breathing and footsteps were heard coming from the court room. Luckily, as I was there, I can say without a shadow of a doubt that when these footsteps were heard no one was in the court room, so where were the phantom footsteps coming from? Part of the area where the cells are situated became an air-raid shelter – its door kept opening on its own. Was something trying to attract our attention? My colleagues shut this door many times during the night and then stood back to observe it opening, seemingly by itself. We questioned what it could have been, and a sensitive-to-spirit member informed us that there was the spirit of a jailer with us and he opened and closed the door regularly; apparently we were not the only ones who had experienced this phenomenon.

Strangely, after the investigation but before the report was published, a gentleman contacted the team to say that he had worked at the Old Crown Court and cells for a couple of years, and he mentioned that he used to observe the spirit of a gentleman in the cells area who would open and close the doors. We were amazed as it was not possible that he could have known what we had experienced during our investigation. He also reported that he had heard men's voices in the court room when the area was empty, and the sound of keys jangling in the holding area outside the cells. The most spectacular thing he saw was a bright light hovering above the dock, located in the centre of the court room. He observed the light for around thirty seconds before it disappeared and he could find no logical explanation for it. He described it as looking similar to a spotlight but hovering in mid-air above the dock. Could this have been the spirit of someone awaiting their fate from the judge?

June visited the Old Crown Courts and cells in 2006 and had no idea that a paranormal investigation had taken place there. In fact, she admitted that, even though history fascinated her, she had no real interest in the paranormal or anything to do with ghosts. She joined the tour late one afternoon and wanted to take some photographs. She and a friend hung to the back of the group, which consisted of approximately twelve people. June admits that as she was at the back of the group, she did not hear much of what the tour guide was saying as she was more interested in who or what was following her. When she stopped to take a photograph, she felt someone physically bump into her, and not realising another member of the tour was behind her when she stopped so suddenly, she swung round to make her apologies but to her amazement there was no one there. She thought nothing of it and tried to focus her digital camera – without success. The group started to move on and so June followed, still fiddling with her camera. Behind her she heard someone drop their keys and again turned around to see who it was. Again there was no one there and as she glanced at the rest of the group ahead of her she realised that none of them seemed to have heard the sound. Seconds later she heard a loud groaning sound close to her right ear. This made her jump and all the hairs on the back of her neck seemed to stand up on end. She swung around, this time a little more scared, believing someone was playing a joke on her. No one was there and she ran on to catch up with the group. After the tour finished, June told a member of staff about what she had experienced. He admitted he had never felt anything untoward during the time he worked there, but he did tell the women that a month or two earlier a paranormal group had been to the Old Crown Courts and experienced similar things.

June went home and searched the internet for 'Old Crown Courts and cells' paranormal experiences. When she did this she found SP UK's website and was able to read how similar her experiences were to theirs. She strongly believes to this day that she and the tour group were being followed when visiting the Old Crown Court.

The Old Crown Court and cells are only accessible when you take part in a tour by an experienced guide, who will bring the court's gruesome history alive for you. It is well worth a visit and you will not be disappointed.

Old Queen Vic

The Kings Arms Hotel on High East Street is impressive at night, standing like a beacon on the street. Built in 1720, it was sympathetically refurbished in 2006 but it has retained many of its classical and stunning Georgian features. Over the years it has accommodated notables including the Beatles and the Rolling Stones, and as the hotel's name suggests it has also played host to some of our country's most significant royals, including King George IV and Queen Victoria. Tales of paranormal activity can be sketchy and at times so fanciful that it is hard to believe or make sense of them. However, when you talk to those who have made these claims, many seem believable however ridiculous they sound on paper – this is one such story.

A woman in her fifties was on business in Dorchester and booked in for two nights at the Kings Arms. As the hotel bill was being paid for by her company, she booked one of the four-poster bedrooms. The room was beautiful and after the first day of business she was glad to return to the hotel for a home-cooked meal in the comfortable restaurant, before retiring to her room for the evening. Whilst she was soaking in the jacuzzi, she heard the door to her room opening – her first instinct was to think it was housekeeping, though she did think it was a little odd that they had not knocked first; it was also very late. She called out to the mysterious visitor but there was no reply, and as she could still hear movement in the room she got out of the bath and grabbed her dressing gown. As she did so, there was an almighty bang from the bedroom area. She rushed in as it sounded as though someone had either dropped something heavy or knocked over a chair or large item of furniture. When she got into the room she could not believe her eyes – nothing was out of place and there was definitely no one in the room. A bit bemused she made her way back to the bathroom after checking the door to her room was still locked. She got back into the bath and continued to soak. However, a couple of minutes later she heard the sounds again. No one was there but she could still hear banging noises in the room. A little incensed, she rang reception to ask if they could possibly tell the people in the room next to her to be a little quieter – it was now nearing 11 p.m. and she had to be up early the next morning. However, reception told her that the adjacent rooms were vacant and they were not expecting guests for those rooms until the next day. As she put the phone down the lights in the room started to flicker as if there was an electrical disturbance. She unlocked the room door and looked down the corridor, observing the lighting there was normal. She went back in to her room and turned the lights off and then back on and they returned to normal.

Breathing a sigh of relief she returned to the bathroom which had the distinct smell of roses. The noises in the bedroom began again, accompanied by a waft of icy-cold air. She decided to retire to bed, but no sooner had she settled down when the television appeared to turn itself on. Thinking it may have been on a timer from the last guest, she unplugged it from the wall socket and returned back to her warm bed. The room was still icy cold even though the radiators were on full. What seemed like a couple of minutes later she felt a tug on the bed clothes which she felt were being pulled off. Desperate to keep warm, and half asleep, she held on for dear life, not really realising what was happening. She could not win the battle though, and seconds later the covers were tugged strongly out of her grasp. She sat bolt upright to find the covers

The Kings Arms Hotel where the ghost of Queen Victoria may disturb your bath.

crumpled on the floor at the end of the bed. She was wide awake now, not only confused but freezing cold. She had to rub her eyes several times as she swore she could see a mist forming, and at first presumed it was because her eyes were sleepy, but after rubbing them she could still see the mist. Slowly and before her eyes she could see the shape of a woman appear. After a couple of minutes she realised that this figure, with its a round face and flattened, centrally parted hair scooped up back behind her head, and dressed in grey, regal clothing, was Queen Victoria. The figure stared as though she was shocked to see the woman in the bed. After a couple of minutes, the lady in the bed said 'hello m'am'. At this point the image started to slowly fade and then completely disappeared.

The businesswoman got up and checked out. She made it to her meeting early that day, and since the event she has told two other people about what happened in the hotel that night. Of all the accounts I have been given over the years, it is one of the most believable I have heard and where did we discuss it? Where else but over a coffee in the Kings Arms Hotel of course!

The Rattling Napper

The Nappers Mite restaurant is located on South Street and welcomes holiday makers and locals all year round to dine in truly historic surroundings. The building that now houses the restaurant was built in 1613 by Sir Robert Napper to house ten old men shortly after the fire that swept through the town. Set around a small courtyard, with a stunning old clock over the entrance, it is the oldest building in South Street and one of the most enchanting places to eat in Dorchester. It is in the kitchen of this restaurant that cutlery is said to fly to the floor for no apparent reason, and an old gentleman has been seen lurking in the courtyard late at night after the restaurant is closed. Could the figure be one of the men that were housed in the almshouse, still residing here in spirit? The phenomenon was reported approximately five years ago in the months of June and July. The chef at the time came to work one morning to find the cutlery that was cleaned the night before was scattered over the floor. He picked it all up but as soon as he turned his back he heard an enormous clatter and turned round to find the entire rack of cutlery back on the floor. Was someone playing games with him? Less than a month later one of the waiters, after a long evening shift, closed the doors of the restaurant and started to clean the courtyard tables. He knew he and his manager were the only two people in the building as the others had gone home, and so you can imagine his surprise when he turned around to see an old gentleman by one of the tables. His first instinct was to tell the gentleman that the restaurant was closed, but before he had the chance to speak the gentleman seemed to fade before completely disappearing. The employee had only seen the figure briefly, but described him as wearing old, dark clothing and had a long beard and unkempt hair, and carrying a walking stick. When the waiter ran in to tell his manager he felt foolish but was even more surprised to learn the history of the building and the purpose for which it was built.

Bridging the Gap

Dorchester West Railway Station, opened in 1857, is one of two stations in Dorchester town and has two platforms. It is very different from its bustling sister station, Dorchester South.

Dorchester West is unmanned and generally a much quieter station on the outskirts of the town. The footbridge at the station carries the

Nappers Mite, still a home for many spectral figures.

identification marker WEY209161M61CH, which indicates that it is bridge 209 on the Weymouth line, located 161 miles and 61 chains from London Paddington. It is on this footbridge that over twenty people in the last five years have witnessed what appears to be a similar apparition of a gentleman. Does this bridge literally bridge the gap not only between station platforms but between our world and the spirit world? The reports of the gentleman on the bridge are almost all identical – the figure appears out of nowhere and walks towards the observer and then passes by. When the astounded onlooker turns around they see him as normal, as he walks down the steps to the platform, where he disappears. When they then look over the side of the bridge to see the bottom of the steps, he is nowhere to be seen. He is well-dressed in a dark-coloured frock coat with a waistcoat underneath and hat that most of the witnesses described as being of the late-nineteenth-century period. He also carries a small, black briefcase-style bag under one arm, is clean shaven with neat black hair, and wears small, dark-rimmed glasses. Some people report that he smiles kindly at them as he passes by. His dress fits into the period when the station was built. Martine's *Handbook of Etiquette and Guide to True Politeness* by Arthur Martine, first published in 1866, confirmed this by saying:

> The dress of a gentleman should be such as not to excite any special observation, unless it be for neatness and propriety. The utmost care should be exercised to avoid even the appearance of desiring to attract attention by the peculiar formation of any article of attire, or by the display of an immoderate quantity of jewellery, both being a positive evidence of vulgarity. His dress should be studiously neat, leaving no other impression than that of a modern well dressed gentleman. There are four kinds of coats which he must have: a business coat, a frock coat, a dress-coat and an overcoat. A well dressed gentleman may do well with four of the first, and one each of the others per annum. An economical gentleman may get by with less.

Where does this spectre come from and why does he appear in front of people? One possible explanation is that the bridge could hold some sort of portal or vortex between our world and the spirit world. A portal or vortex is believed to be a spiritual inter-dimensional gateway or doorway between worlds that are invisible to the living human eye. This cannot be proved but the fact that this gentleman has been seen so regularly tells its own story. It could be that he was a regular visitor to this station when he was alive, possibly making the same journey for many years. Perhaps the spirit of a gentleman is simply reliving over and over again the route he took to work or home.

At first you may assume that this is a tape-recording-theory sighting, a recording of a time gone; however, on closer inspection of the reports, it seems unlikely. One thing that makes this unlikely is the apparent interaction he has with the people he is passing. Some say he nods or smiles, whilst some say he passes without looking at them at all.

Paranormal recordings do not interact with the witnesses as they are not spirits, but as the name suggests, spiritual recordings. Just in the same way, when you are watching a video or DVD, the cast of the film do not interact with the audience as it is not a live performance, but pre-recorded. This is possibly a repetition sighting as the gentleman seems to be reliving the moment over and over again. Often the spirit is distressed, although certainly not in this case.

Spirit of Casterbridge

Hardy's novel, *The Mayor of Casterbridge*, was set in Dorchester, Casterbridge being its fictional name. In the story, Henchard, the mayor, attended official meetings at the Casterbridge Hotel located in High Street East.

The Station Pub, where you may not be alone – even in the toilet!

The fictitional inn was based on the Kings Arms, although at the time that Hardy wrote the *Mayor of Casterbridge* the inn was a Georgian house. The building has retained many period features, including a concealed courtyard annexe.

Downstairs the ghost of a lady has been seen on several occasions and it is believed she is related to the building before it became a hotel. She is said to have a pale face and long, flowing blonde hair, and is seen looking out of the French doors; observers have nicknamed her Emily. She only appears for seconds at a time and poses no threat. Those who have seen her say she is a calming influence on them, making them feel at ease and at peace.

The Spirit of a Restaurant

(Historical information taken from www.wikipedia.org)

George Darrell Jeffreys was born in 1648. Educated at Cambridge, he was appointed Solicitor General to the Duke of York and was knighted in 1677.

He became recorder of London in 1678, and by the time he was thirty-three he became Lord Chief Justice of England and a privy counsellor, later becoming Lord Chancellor. In 1683, he became Baron Jeffreys of Wem. In the West Country, Judge Jeffreys is remembered for the part he played in the Bloody Assizes which followed the Monmouth Rebellion in 1685, arriving in Dorchester and lodging at No.6 High West Street while he presided over trials in the region. Legend has it that he was more often drunk than sober and had an unpredictable temper. He would rant and rave at those unfortunate enough to be brought before him, and subsequently the Dorchester trials became known as the bloodiest of the assizes.

The events leading up to the Bloody Assizes started on 11 June 1685 when James, Duke of Monmouth, the illegitimate son of Charles II and pretender to the throne, landed at Lyme Regis. He made his way to Taunton in Somerset with his small band of followers, rallying support along the way, and it was there that he was declared king and presented with flags embroidered by the maids of Taunton, pupils of Mistress Susanna Musgrave and Mistress Mary Blake. The rebellious uprising was a disaster and it was only a matter of weeks before James was captured, taken to London and executed.

The assizes started at Winchester on 25 August 1685 when the king declared that all followers and supporters of the Duke of Monmouth and his rebellion should be put on trial. There were five judges – Baron Montagu, Baron Wright, Justice Wythens, Justice Levinz and Sir Henry Polexfen, led by Lord Chief Justice Jeffreys. It was in Winchester that the trial of Dame Alice Lyle took place and from Winchester they proceeded to Dorchester where local men were put on trial for the parts they played in or the support they pledged to the Monmouth Rebellion. The trials were nicknamed bloody for a reason, as while many supporters were sentenced to fines or transportation, many others were also hung, drawn and quartered or beheaded. Heads were then placed on the railings of the local churches to display a warning to all who choose to support a rebellion. Whilst conducting these trials he lodged in High West Street close to where he was to hold court. It is believed that the judge did not want to travel far from his lodgings to be able to do this and he did not want to have to mix in with the locals, so he used a tunnel connected to his lodgings, wide enough for two or three people to walk side by side to get directly to his court room in a building behind where he lodged. The building in which he lodged is still in use today and is aptly named The Judge Jeffreys Restaurant.

Jeffreys returned to London after the assizes to report to the King, where he was rewarded for his loyalty to the Crown and made Lord

Home to the infamous Judge Jeffreys in death, as it was in life.

Chancellor. However, he died in 1689 in his mid-forties. Even though his death was recorded in London, local legend dictates that his body was walled up in the lodgings in Dorchester for his evil deeds against the locals. Since this day it is said that he haunts his former lodgings, banging and moving objects in temper, and pacing up and down on the wooden floors. It is rumoured that on some nights if you look up at the windows of the restaurant from the High Street, you can see the judge's wigged head, with his dark eyes staring back at you.

It is unlikely that the legend of him being walled up is true, and was probably a story created to enable the townspeople to feel that justice had been done. The ghost of Judge Jeffreys is said to be seen all over the south of the country; in fact, in most of the places he visited or held court, they claim to have his ghost. Perhaps he visits all his former haunts just to let us know he is still around, trying to assert the power he once had over the people.

The Ghosts of Antelope Walk

Antelope Walk is situated in Cornhill and is a quaint shopping arcade imaginatively transformed using the entrance and courtyard of the old Antelope Hotel, an eighteenth-century coaching inn and a great rival, at the time, of the Kings Arms. The walk now houses many small local businesses including the Celtic Kitchen, the Teddy Bear House, the Bridge Flower Shop and the Oak Tea Room. As the popularity of travelling increased in the sixteenth and seventeenth centuries, the importance of inns such as the Antelope grew. In the early 1800s the hotel became a main stop on the London, Bath, Bristol and Exeter routes and was used by coaches on a daily basis. It is believed that on some nights, famous coaches such as the Magnet, the John Bull and the Duke of Wellington can still be seen and heard rumbling over the cobbles of the Antelope Hotel, bringing phantom travellers from all over the south of the country to Dorset's county town for business and pleasure. If you are ever walking down Cornhill and past the Antelope Walk late at night, spare a quick glance into the darkness and see if you are still able to see or hear any ghostly tourists arriving in the town.

The Oak Tea Room, which dates back to 1589 and bridges the walkway, is another location in Antelope Walk that is said to be haunted by unruly spirits. A former employee of the tea rooms explained that, on many occasions, invisible voices and mumbling could be heard, even when the shop was shut. Items of furniture would also be moved by invisible hands overnight and staff would come in the next day to find chairs on the tables, and items such as crockery rearranged from the way it was left the night before. She also said that if the tea room was empty, it would feel as though it was full, and that unseen eyes were watching. The tea room has a peaceful and relaxed feeling to it on most days and yet occasionally, when all the visitors have left, the atmosphere feels heavy and oppressive for no apparent reason. Despite all the reported sightings from employees past and present, happenings seem to occur when the building has closed. One ex-employee said that she once felt as though she was surrounded by masculine energy, as though all her actions were being observed and scrutinised. It is hard to imagine who would haunt this charming little

The cobbled entrance to Antelope Walk where ghostly carriages have been heard.

The courtyard of Antelope Walk where the ghost of Judge Jeffreys may still be seen making his way to his court room.

tea room, but, when you look further back into the history of Antelope Walk, it all becomes disturbingly clear.

The final part of Antelope Walk that is apparently haunted is the inn's former courtyard which is now situated approximately halfway up the walk. During the Bloody Assizes the notorious Judge Jeffreys entered the courtroom directly from his lodgings by a tunnel that connected the two. The court room was the Oak Room of the former Antelope Hotel, and it was here that 312 local men were put on trial and sentenced by Jeffreys to be fined, whipped, and transported, or in seventy-four cases, to be executed. It is said that the judge, to this day, still haunts the courtyard of the inn and so is it possible that he still haunts the nearby Oak Tea Room? The courtyard haunting is so well known locally, that there is even a sign in Antelope Way that tells of the area's ghost; however, that does not explain the feeling of multiple presences in the tea room. I spoke to John, a local businessman who has an interesting view about what else may haunt the tea room. He believes that the spirits of the men who were sentenced to death are the ones that can be felt in the Oak Room, trapped here due to their feelings of injustice and scorned by unfairness. In turn he believes that the spirit of the judge, not trapped in his former surroundings, returns here in visitation almost as a taunt to those men and the power he once had over them.

The Souls of some of Dorchester's Oldest Residents

Maumbury Rings is one of Dorchester's most popular natural visitor attractions and is located just south of the town centre, between Weymouth Avenue and Maumbury Road. It is a Neolithic henge dating from around 2,500 BC, and its banks, which are almost circular, have a diameter of over 100m with a single entrance at the north-east. The earthworks are recorded as ancient monuments and have three clear phases of construction. In AD 100, like many Neolithic sites in England, the Roman Army of Durnovaria adapted the site to form an amphitheatre. Maumbury is one of the largest recorded sites of this kind. They removed earth from the centre of the rings and used it to create tiered levels by piling it on the existing Neolithic bank.

Amphitheatres were the centre of entertainment in the Roman period where citizens went to watch gladiatorial fights and where criminals had to fight for their lives. The crowds roaring from Maumbury Rings would have been heard for miles. Despite its popularity at the time, the amphitheatre went out of use in AD 150.

Between 1642 and 1643, during the English Civil War, the Maumbury site was remodelled into an artillery fort guarding the southern approach to Dorchester. In 1705, a crowd of over 18,000 curious people gathered at the rings to see the alleged Dorchester murderess, Mary Channing, put to death. She was forced into a loveless marriage; however, her husband then died of poisoning and Mary, who was nicknamed the 'she wolf', was prosecuted as it was apparently proved beyond reasonable doubt that she was his killer. She was brought to Maumbury where she was strangled and burned for her crime in front of the bloodthirsty crowd. As the legend goes, if you visit the rings in the late evening, the time of Mary's execution, her screams can still be heard, reliving her execution for eternity.

The rings have continued to interest antiquarians since the seventeenth century, and in 1903 a series of excavations began on the rings. These revealed animals' skulls and other interesting artefacts that charted the rings' history. Most of these are now on display at the Dorset Museum. Does something else remain at the rings waiting to be discovered?

The town's police station stands immediately next to the ring complex and so not surprisingly the first of the sightings was recorded by a policeman in 1991. He finished his shift at midnight and headed home on foot, turning left out of the main entrance as usual. As he passed the gate for the rings, he heard noises from within the complex and decided to go in to check out what was happening. As he got close to the north-east entrance the voices were getting louder, and whilst he could not hear what they were shouting, he worried that it may be an organised fight and quickened his pace. As he approached the entrance he could see inside the earthworks and naked flames flickering in the dark night. The flames seemed not only to be in the centre but also around the edges. He panicked, thinking that some children may have started lots of small bonfires. He entered the henge and was just reaching for the torch that he kept in his rucksack when silence fell. He looked up and the fires had disappeared. He stood for a couple of minutes absorbing the silence around him. There was no one around and the only sounds he could hear were the faint hum of cars from the town centre and the wind blowing through the trees behind him. What he saw next was enough to make even the most sceptical person think twice. Out of the corner of his eye he caught sight of someone. In the dim light the figure appeared to be that of a middle-aged gentleman. His clothes were tattered and shredded, and he was swaying as he ran, his bent-over body unable to keep in a straight line. Worried that the figure approaching had been attacked in some way and was injured, the policeman walked towards him. The figure suddenly collapsed on the grass, only 2ft away from the policeman, and then disappeared. The policeman dropped to his knees and started to feel around on the ground – he knew that feeling around for the gentleman was absurd as he saw him disappear, but he admits his brain could not comprehend what he had seen and so he assumed his eyes were playing tricks on him. When he found nothing, he remembered the fires he had seen earlier. Not satisfied that they had also just disappeared, he got up and started to climb the west henge to find evidence that they had been there. He found nothing to suggest that any fire had been there at all, let alone minutes ago. Determined to find sense in what he had witnessed, he walked the entire henge complex but still found nothing. By now it was after 12.30 a.m. and he decided to go straight home. He reported the event to his colleagues, although he chose not to reveal certain incidents. He said he had heard voices and a commotion which had made him

Does the bleeding man still roam this entrance to Maumbury Rings?

go and investigate, and that he had seen a gentleman who appeared to be injured but ran off. The rest of the story he has kept secret for over eighteen years, until now. He is now retired from the police force but says he will never forget that night. He said:

> It was the most incredibly unreal moment of my life. My wife thought I was having some sort of breakdown as I could not talk much and just kept shaking my head in disbelief for hours after. Whoever that gentleman was and whatever he was doing, I will never forget him, I am just sorry I could not help him. If people out there do not believe, then they need to spend a night at the rings. If they see what I saw then they would have no choice but to believe.

The Boys of the Borough

The seventeenth-century Borough Arms on High East Street nestles amongst the larger buildings that surround it. In the early twentieth century, a group of men used to meet at the pub to discuss business in the town. All local traders, they became known as the Borough Boys. The group was led by James Briggs, a butcher, and the group are said to haunt the pavement outside the pub. I spoke to James's great grandson, Jed, who said he and his family are very proud of his great grandfather and as a family they still meet and drink at the pub. Some evenings the ghosts of James and his men have been seen congregating outside the pub ready for their meeting. Jed explained that, as far as they know, James and his fellow traders used to meet outside and only enter the inn when they were all there. The sightings that have been reported have always mentioned seven men and when the eighth spectral figure arrives the group vanishes, so we can perhaps assume there were eight men in the group. Inside the inn, laughing has been heard coming from empty tables, and items have been known to move about, although a member of staff mentioned that nothing has ever been broken. The rest of the staff remain sceptical that the pub is haunted as they have not witnessed anything unusual.

The Ghost of St Peter's Church

Built from Portland and Ham Hill stone, St Peter's Church dominates the town centre and stands where High West Street, High East Street and Cornhill meet. The present church dates to 1454 (a church is recorded

Does the Borough Arms continue as a meeting place for the spirits of local businessmen?

St Peter's Church in Dorchester's town centre.

The aisle of St Peter's Church where the ghost of angry Revd Nathaniel Templeman has been sighted.

on the site before 1454) and has connections with Thomas Hardy (who helped to restructure it in the fifteenth century), poet William Barnes, the Earl of Shaftesbury and Lord Holles. Despite its welcoming appearance it appears to be haunted by the spirit of a former vicar, Revd Nathaniel Templeman, who appears to be quite unhappy. Templeman's ghost first appeared in the church a couple of months after his death in 1814. It was Christmas Eve and the new vicar had left the task of decorating the church to the sexton, Ambrose Hunt, and the church warden, Clerk Hardy. Templeman had been a popular and long-serving vicar and so they wanted to make this first Christmas service without him extra special. After a couple of hours of work in the cold church they finally had it ready for the next day's event. Tired, the two men decided to help themselves to a glass of communion wine, and settled down in the pews to admire their handy work. It is said that as they sat there, the ghost of Revd Templeman appeared, walking towards them and waving his fists in rage. The two men said he had a look of sheer anger in his eyes and his mouth was opening and closing as though he was shouting, but the men could hear nothing. Hardy was so shocked he was said to faint, while Hunt dropped to his knees and started reciting the *Lord's Prayer*. As he did this he tentatively looked up and Templeman paused and then drifted away down the north aisle from where he eventually vanished. As soon as the ghost had gone, Hunt jumped to his feet and ran to a nearby inn to tell his story, leaving Hardy where he lay. Many of the inn's patrons ran to the church to see if they could spot the angry ghost but all they found was a mumbling Hardy lying on the floor where he had fallen. Speculation suggested that Templeman was angry with the men for drinking the communion wine; some even said that the effect of the wine on the men had caused them to see the ghost.

The ghost of Templeman was, however, seen many times after this and each time appeared angry and in a rage, silently shouting at people, although no reports were as clear as Hunt and Hardy's. Until the day the men died they never changed their stories and were able to describe the ghost in great detail, having seen him at a distance of less than 10ft away. Clearly distressed about something, if Templeman does get his message across, then maybe one day he will be able to move on.

two

Dorchester – Suburbs and Surrounding Areas

The Tuneful Barrows

Impressive long barrows are situated along the ridgeway between Dorchester and Weymouth. At certain times of the year these barrows apparently emit strange ethereal singing sounds and have been nicknamed by locals as the 'Singing Marys'. Local legend suggests they are the ancient voices of the dead buried within the barrows. In an effort to diffuse this theory, scientists and antiquarians (including the famous antiquarian John Aubrey, 1626-1697) have investigated over the years but no satisfactory explanation has been found for this strange phenomena.

The Black Lady of the A35

The A35 is the main route from Bournemouth and Poole to Dorchester. On a section of the road close to the village of Puddletown Forest, a black lady has sometimes been seen. She moves towards the road, stopping briefly, before stepping out onto the carriageway and sometimes into the path of an oncoming vehicle. One lorry driver has seen this figure, witnessing her twice now on the exact same part of the road. Brian, who has worked for thirty-four years for a nationally recognised company,

The phantom motorcyclist has been heard in this quiet lay-by near Dorchester.

regularly uses the A35 transporting garden goods between the company depot in London and his home town of Dorchester. He has night driven on the continent and in the UK and so is used to driving at night and in the dark, and believes his eyes have now become adjusted to it. He admits to having seen many strange things; however, he is a logical person with a scientific brain and can usually explain what he has seen. On the two occasions he has seen the black lady, however, he cannot find a logical explanation. The first time he encountered her, he thought the figure was a deer on the side of the road. He pulled into the second lane hoping that the animal would decide to stay put and not run out in front of him. When he got a little closer to the shape he saw that it was now standing up. He laughed as he recalled how he thought it was odd that a deer was standing on its hind legs. However, he soon saw the features on the figure and realised it was a woman, heading across the road and into his lane. Fortunately, because of the time at night, there was little other traffic on the road and so he was able to slam on his brakes, but it was not soon enough, and as the shape crossed in front of him, it disappeared under the lorry, or so Brian thought. When he was able to safely stop, he walked back along the grass verge to where he believed he had hit the woman. He was shaken and his mind raced as he truly believed he had run someone down. When he got to the place in the road where the incident had occurred, there was nothing there. He took his key-ring torch from his pocket and quickly scanned the area but he could still not see anything out of the ordinary, let alone a body of any kind. Even more shaken now and a little bit spooked, he gingerly returned to his lorry, looking around constantly as he made his way back. He sat for a while and contemplated what had happened. He admits that he was now scared by what he had seen and did not sit for long before starting his journey again. When he reached the Dorchester store it was starting to get light and he had had a little while to think about what had happened. He was so sure he had hit something but one thing bothered him – why had he not felt or heard the impact? He could not make sense of it and it took him a couple of days to get his head around what he had seen.

That was just over three years ago and up until a month or so ago he had tried not to give it much thought – that was until he found himself on the same stretch of road again in the early hours one Friday. As he approached the Puddletown Forest turn off, he saw there was no oncoming traffic on the road ahead and so he turned his lights on full beam. As he passed the turning he looked up the road and his heart skipped a beat when he glanced at the side of the road. If he had not been driving he said he would have rubbed his eyes, as he felt as though he was dreaming. Just ahead of him, to his left on the same bit of verge as before, was the shadowy figure that he recognised all too well. As he approached, the figure stood up and made a move to the road. This time the night was clear and there was almost a full moon, and Brian clearly saw the ashen figure with long, dark hair. He slammed on his breaks, but again it was too late to make an immediate stop and he watched the shadowy figure appear in front of him before seemingly disappearing under the lorry again. This time he was prepared and listened – there was indeed no impact and he felt nothing. This time he did not stop, although he admits to glancing out of the wing mirror.

This phenomenon appears to be an anniversary haunting, occurring at the same time of year. Brian is sure he will see her again some day as he often drives on that stretch of road, but he is in two minds about it. He is intrigued, but at the same time finds it all very strange.

Who was the woman, and what was her story? Was she killed on this busy road and will she continue to walk this particular stretch of road for eternity?

The Phantom Motorcyclist

The A35 is a long stretch of road and there are only a few areas on it where you are able to stop for rest or a toilet break. There is a lay-by next to some trees and it is here that a phantom motorcyclist has been heard by the toilet block. During the day, motorists stopping would not give the area a second thought; however, at night this area takes on a different atmosphere and is scarily dark, especially with the woods so close by.

One late night in November, a couple from Lyme Regis were heading up the A35 to visit relatives in Ferndown, near Ringwood, and they decided to stop at the lay-by. The husband pulled into a parking space facing the woods and the woman was quick to jump out of the car, joking to her husband that if she was not back in ten minutes he was to come and look for her. It was a cold and frosty night and so she ran quickly to the ladies' toilet. Suddenly, she heard the roar of a motorbike in the car park. When she came out of the cubicle she was glad to hear the motorcyclist had gone and she heard him heading off into the distance.

When she got back into the car, she asked her husband what the motorbike rider had been doing. He looked at her blankly, and said 'what motorbike?' He could not even remember a car passing the lay-by let alone a motorbike. The woman laughed as she was sure that he was teasing her. However two years later, he swears that no motorbike came into or even passed the lay-by that night.

After a little research, I discovered that the ghostly figure of a motorcyclist has been seen in or close to the lay-by before. It was seen by an off-duty policeman who saw the man as he passed the lay-by one evening. He said the rider was dressed in black leather and wearing a dull-blue motorcycle helmet. The policeman was concerned, as he could not see the motorcyclist's bike anywhere, and so he pulled in to see if he could offer any assistance. When he turned in to the parking area, the motorcycle and rider had disappeared. The only conclusion the policeman could come to is that he had run into the woods behind the lay-by, but it was autumn and the trees were virtually bare, yet he could see no one in them. Confused, he continued on his journey.

The Tolpuddle Horses

Not only famous for the Tolpuddle Martyrs, the village is well known for the phantom horses that appear to roam its streets. The name of the

The Martyrs Inn at Tolpuddle is home to phantom horses.

village is derived from a woman who lived in the era of Edward the Confessor called Tole. Together with her husband she was a benefactor to Abbotsbury Abbey, the land of which belonged to the Manor of Tolpuddle. On cold winters' nights locals have reported the sound of phantom hooves on the streets of the sleepy village, and the sound of horses have been heard around the Martyrs Inn on the main street in the middle of the night.

A gentleman who was walking his dog in the 1990s reported how his pet appeared confused and spooked by the sound as they walked past the inn. Even though the present building dates to the twentieth century, there has been a coaching inn on this site since the seventeenth century. Perhaps the horses are revisiting their journey to the old coaching inn.

Six Men and a Tree

Between 1770 and 1830, Britain's rural landscape changed drastically. Landowners annexed vast areas of land and acquired great wealth from their new acreage. Peasants had little land on which to grow vegetables or to graze their small animals, and working conditions were poor with low wages. Families became poverty stricken unless they could send their sons, daughters and wives out to work. Severe winters caused further hardship in 1829 and 1830 which fuelled anger among the farm workers, and riots broke out led by the notorious but mythical Captain Swing. During these riots, 600 men were imprisoned, 500 sentenced to be transported and nineteen were executed. In early 1834, six men from Tolpuddle – George Loveless, James Loveless, James Brine, James Hammett, Thomas Stansfield and John Stansfield – all farm labourers, met at Thomas Stansfield's cottage one night along with other labourers. All lived in poverty and George Loveless took it upon himself to form the Friendly Society of Agricultural Labourers, a union to give the labourers more strength when bargaining for better conditions and more pay. James Frampton was a local landowner and, supported by the government at the time, was determined to destroy the unions and what they stood for. He had witnessed the French Revolution and he was resolute that no uprising should threaten or undermine landowners.

The six men regularly met under a sycamore tree in the village, and it is said this site is where they first discussed the possibility of forming a union. At one of those meetings the group were betrayed and news of their union was leaked. On 22 February 1834, posters were erected

The tree where the Tolpuddle Martyrs first hatched their plans to form a union.

The plaque on the martyrs' tree commemorates its place in English history.

threatening villagers with transportation if they were caught joining illegal societies or unions. Two days later, the six men were arrested and taken to the Crown Court cells in Dorchester to await trial.

The Grand Jury's foreman was William Ponsonby MP, and the jury included James Frampton, his stepson Henry, his stepbrother Charles, and several of the magistrates who had signed the arrest warrant. The judge for the trial was Judge Baron Williams, who had made up his mind before even opening the trial by saying, 'The object of all legal punishment is not altogether with the view of operating on the offenders themselves, it is also for the sake of offering an example and a warning to all'.

Edward Legg was the fellow farm labourer who betrayed the men and subsequently they were sentenced to transportation. George Loveless was sent to Tasmania, and the others were sent to Sydney in Australia. An uprising throughout the country followed, and by 1836 the men were fully pardoned and allowed to return to England. George Loveless was the first to return home on 13 June 1837. The others gradually returned, although having felt betrayed by their country most simply collected their families and emigrated to Canada. James Hammett did not return until 1839, and he is the only one of the six that remained in Tolpuddle on his return. He is buried in the local cemetery of St John's Church in the village. The sycamore tree where the men used to meet still stands today and a plaque commemorates the site.

Visitors to Tolpuddle have witnessed the apparition of a male figure under the sycamore tree. He is leaning against its thick trunk, facing the road, and people tend to spot him when they are driving slowly through the village. He does not appear as a solid form but is somewhat misty, and when the observers turn around to drive back past him, he is gone. Locals believe this to be the lonely ghost of James Hammett. With his body so close by in the churchyard, does his spirit make the trip to the tree they used to meet around, in the hope of meeting his five fellow labourers?

I have managed to find a single report of a gentleman seeing six men in nineteenth-century dress standing around the tree one night in February 2003. He was walking his dog along the lane above the green on which the tree stands, and was quite taken aback by the group milling around the tree. As he passed by, the six men apparently looked over towards him. He said he nodded politely and just carried on his way, but, intrigued by the group, he took a quick glance over his shoulder and the men had strangely gone. Have all the Tolpuddle Martyrs eventually been reunited and returned home? If you visit Tolpuddle you may not be able to see the ghosts but you can visit the tree, James Hammett's grave, the cottages where the martyrs lived before they were transported and also the excellent Tolpuddle Martyrs Museum. In July you may well see the martyrs for yourself but they will be actors celebrating the Tolpuddle Martyrs' festival.

The Spirit of Mack's Gate

The National Trust property Max Gate is located in Alington Avenue, approximately one mile out of Dorchester. It was designed by Thomas Hardy and built between 1883 and 1885. A cottage and toll gate used to stand on the site which was occupied by Henry Mack, the turnpike keeper. The cottage was nicknamed Mack's Gate and so when Hardy built his house on the same land he named it Max Gate. When Hardy and his first wife Emma moved in, Emma complained that the house was cold, unfeeling and draughty; her husband, however, just worried about the bills and running costs. The villa was Hardy's home for forty years and remained in his possession until his death in 1928. He completed some of his best and most well-known works in this house, including 900 poems and the novels *Tess of the d'Urbervilles*, *Jude the Obscure* and *The Woodlanders*. The original house that Hardy built was modest in size, but as his career developed he became more stable financially, and was able to afford extensions to the property. Hardy's flair can still be seen in the house as the decor is not too ornate, but instead somewhat understated for its time which is exactly as he wanted it to be. Florence, his second wife, lived with her husband at Max Gate from 1913, and very much made it her home; she seemed a lot happier living in the house than Emma. The home has seen both sadness and happiness over the years and has witnessed many prestigious guests, including Rudyard Kipling, Siegfried Sassoon, H.G. Wells, Robert Louis Stevenson and The Prince of Wales in 1923.

In early 1928 Hardy died at Max Gate and even though his ashes were taken to Westminster and his heart to Stinsford, many people truly believe his soul will remain for eternity in his house. When Florence died the property was auctioned in 1938 and purchased by Hardy's sister, Kate. When she died, she left the house to the National Trust who maintain the property in the way Hardy would have wished. His soul certainly seems to remain in the building as visitors have reported seeing strange shadows and experiencing icy-cold breezes even on the hottest days of the year, and the musty smell of tobacco smoke. It may be assumed that as Hardy built the house it is he who haunts his former home. However, little did he realise when he built the house in 1885 that it was actually situated in the middle of a Neolithic stone circle and later Romano-British cemetery. Perhaps then, the house could be an epicentre of spiritual activity and some believe it is haunted by the spirit of Henry Mack the turnpike keeper. He does not appear to mean anyone any harm – he seems to just watch and follow people around the house when they visit.

Ghostly activity of all kinds at Thorncombe Woods

Thorncombe Woods and Black Heath is a 65-acre site of mixed woodland and heath just north-east of Dorchester. An old Roman road runs through the woods and for centuries it has been said that the footsteps of Roman legionaries can be heard as the ghostly procession continues to march up and down.

Locals had reported a disturbance, and so a local policeman who was patrolling the area at night made his way into the woods. On approaching the old Roman road he heard the sounds of a marching army coming towards

Do you dare sit on this bench on the outskirts of Thorncombe Woods?

him. On investigation he could see nothing, yet the sounds were still clear. The invisible footsteps apparently marched right past him and then faded away. Scared by what he had heard, he quickly scanned the area and left.

Poltergeist activity rarely occurs in buildings so when it is heard in the countryside it is usually viewed with scepticism – that is, until you hear some of the reports from people that have visited the woods.

The area has a large visitor car park, close to which there is a bench where reports of poltergeist activity have been made. When using the bench for resting after a walk, strange and sometimes disturbing things have occurred. Ladies have reported their earrings ripped from their ears with such a force as to cause bleeding. A visitor once reported that he was sitting on the bench and enjoying a drink from a flask of coffee, when it was wrenched from his hands and sent flying onto the ground. When he tried to retrieve the flask it kept rolling just out of his reach. When he was eventually able to reach the flask it was so hot that he was unable to pick it up. A couple of seconds later, he tentatively tried to touch it again and this time it was icy cold. He could not understand what was happening.

Once, a woman was sitting on the bench and put a dish of water on the ground for her terrier dog to have a drink. She then lifted him up in order to clean his feet before returning to her car. Suddenly, the water dish turned over with a crash. At first she thought she had kicked it over herself until she realised that her feet were in fact nowhere near the bowl. Giving no more thought to this, she carried on cleaning the dog. She walked to the rubbish bin to dispose of the tissues she had used on her dog's paws, when she heard him whimper. As she turned round she was shocked to see him levitating above the bench. She rushed over, grabbed him and ran to her car. Once inside she locked all the doors and tried to steady her nerves. It was dusk now and there was only one other car in the car park and no one to be seen anywhere, making her more nervous. Before she had a chance to start the engine, she heard a knocking sound on the rear window. Looking in the rear-view mirror, she saw nothing, and immediately shot the car into reverse.

Needless to say, I do not think that the woman and her dog would have returned to those woods in a hurry.

The Ghosts of Kingston Maurwood

Kingston Maurwood College animal park and gardens is not so well known for its paranormal activity.

Kingston Maurwood.

The house, designed by architect John James of Greenwich, was built between 1717 and 1720 for George Pitt, the cousin of Prime Minister William Pitt. He lived in the building for fourteen years, dying in 1734. George married Laura Grey, a descendant of the Grey family who had acquired the land on which the house was built from the Maurwood family.

Thomas Hardy was a frequent visitor to the house as a boy in the mid-1800s, and in his novel *Desperate Remedies* he referred to Kingston Maurwood as Knapwater House. During the Second World War the house was occupied by American Service men and its extensive grounds were used as a fuel dump for the D-Day landings. According to different sources there may be several ghosts that haunt this beautiful Dorset house. On the top floor, a ghostly woman has been observed descending the back stairs used by the servants. She disappears before she reaches the bottom and it is believed that she was a maid in the house who fell down the stairs, breaking her neck.

A woman in black is one of the most common sightings at the house. In 1998-1999, a young student who was bored during a lecture began to stare out of the window. Suddenly he noticed a woman in a long, dark-coloured dress running quickly across the courtyard. She then appeared to disappear into a solid-brick wall.

Another incident occurred in the summer of 1996 during one of the park's outdoor concerts, when a group of ladies saw a woman in a long, black dress floating above the ground near the front entrance to the house, before disappearing into thin air. Could this be the same maid? Or a former lady of the house?

The ghost of George Pitt is said to haunt the main foyer of the house and has been seen sitting on one of the chairs by the fireplace. Even people that have not seen him have seen his shadow and heard his heavy footsteps on the stone floor. Maybe Pitt, incensed that he only got to spend fourteen years in his house, has returned to enjoy a bit more time in the property he built.

The Headless Grey Lady

Throughout the country there are reports of apparent sightings of infamous grey ladies but the Wolfeton's grey lady is unique, as well as the spirits of two other former residents of the house. A description of the house is taken from the www.touruk.co.uk website:

> Wolfeton House is a fine early Tudor and Elizabethan manor house set in water-meadows near the confluence of the rivers Frome and Cerne. The building is a substantial remnant of the house built by the Trenchards, once one of the leading families in Dorset. The estate passed to John Trenchard by marriage in 1480. He and his son, Thomas Trenchard, built a compact courtyard house on the site. In the late-16th century Sir George Trenchard extended the south range and embellished the building. He added the splendid plaster ceilings, fireplaces and panelling dating from around 1580. This was the peak of Wolfeton's prosperity and from this period onwards the house gradually declined. In the late-18th century Wolfeton House was abandoned by Sir George's descendants

Wolfeton House, where a coach and horses can be seen ascending the main staircase.

and it was later sold to cousins. By 1800 the chapel in the north range was in ruins and in 1822 - 28 other parts of the house were demolished. In 1862 the property was purchased by W.H.P. Weston who repaired the remaining buildings and carried out some modifications. The present owner is a kinsman of the Trenchard family and since 1973 he has carried out further restoration to the house. Wolfeton House is approached through the medieval Gatehouse that was once attached to north and south ranges of the early Tudor house. This led through to the small courtyard of the Trenchard's house.

The first sighting of a ghost at Wolfeton house was reported by Judge Thomas Trenchard. One evening, Thomas and his wife were dining with guests when Thomas was reputed to have looked up and seen a ghostly vision of his wife standing behind one of the guests. The figure was an exact replica of her, only there were blood stains over her grey, velvet dress and she was carrying her severed head under her arm.

Thomas was obviously shocked and did not tell his wife what he had seen. Lady Trenchard took her own life that very evening by cutting her own throat. Was the apparition sent to warn Thomas of his wife's impending demise? Her ghost, headless or sometimes carrying her severed head, has frequently been seen in the house and has been nicknamed the headless grey lady.

Another ghost said to roam Wolfeton House, its gatehouse and grounds, is said to be the spirit of an Irish Catholic priest called Cornelius. He was once a regular guest at the house but was hung, drawn and quartered in Dorchester for crimes against the church. It is believed that Wolfeton house is where he was finally captured. Perhaps this is why he appears to return to the gatehouse time and time again. He was first seen on the staircase of the gatehouse but his footsteps can also be heard as he keeps returning to the room in which he used to stay.

The third ghost is said to be that of Thomas Trenchard. It is claimed he won a large amount of money whilst drinking with friends and completing a bet. After he bragged about the size of the staircase at Wolfeton House, his friends wagered that he could not get a horse and coach up it. Not one to be beaten, Trenchard proved them wrong by saddling up his horses, attaching a coach and driving it up the staircase for his friends' amusement. Apparently to this day his victorious ghost reportedly re-enacts the antics of that drunken night and a ghostly coach and horses can be seen climbing the great staircase with Thomas at the reins.

Dorchester's Most Haunted Building

Every region has a place that they consider the most paranormally active in the area and Dorset's has to be Athelhampton House (also referred to as Athelhampton Hall by locals), situated seven miles to the East of Dorchester. The impressive building you see today has been built over five centuries thus creating one of the finest fifteenth-century manor houses in England. The Athelhampton House website, www.athelhampton.co.uk, tells the interesting story of the rise of one of Dorset's most popular tourist attractions.

The land the house is built on has been inhabited since 1086 and in 1485 the great hall, solar and buttery were constructed by Sir William Martyn. Sir Martyn, who was a local man from a well-known Dorset family, was Lord Mayor of London at the time. In the second half of the sixteenth century, Robert Martyn built the west wing and gatehouse and shortly after a separate building was erected to the rear of the main property, and the house was divided into four separate dwellings. When

Athelhampton House.

Nicholas Martyn died in 1595, the family estate was divided among his four daughters and by 1665 the house had a new owner, Sir Robert Long. Like many other properties at the time, the buildings started to fall in to disrepair and in 1848 it was sold to George Wood. In 1862 Wood demolished the gatehouse. Members of Thomas Hardy's family worked on the restoration and Athelhampton became immortalised in two of Hardy's poems of that time. In 1891, the well-known antiquarian Alfred de Lafontaine began a major restoration of the gardens creation of the formal gardens with designer by Iniago Thomas. Their aim was to create a series of outdoor rooms in the grounds inspired by the renaissance. The most recent addition to the house was as recent as 1920 when a North Wing was constructed by owner George Cockrane. In 1957, Athelhampton was purchased by Robert Victor Cooke who brought in much of the period furniture you see in the house today. He also made further improvements to the gardens before he left it to his son MP Sir Robert Cooke. The house has stayed in the family and in 1995, when his father passed away Patrick Cooke and his wife Andrea took over the running of Athelhampton and are the current owners.

Athelhampton Hall has been used by the media for filming projects including *Sleuth*, *Doctor Who*, *Grass Roots*, *Going for Song* and *Most Haunted*.

One of the most prolific ghosts at Athelhampton is the spirit of a pet ape which belonged to a member of the Martyn family in the sixteenth century, and is said to still roam the rooms of the house. When the Martyn line ceased in 1595, the ape was left trapped in a secret passageway leading off the great hall, and he died there. The ape's ghost is now said to search the house in vain looking for his master. On some nights his cry can be heard in the great hall and a thudding sound is clearly audible on the staircase, close to the entrance to the secret passageway.

Another ghost pet that resides at Athelhampton is that of a gardener's cat. In 1957, Mr Cooke, the owner at the time, could hear the padding of cat's paws on the wooden floor of the great stairway. He caught sight of the cat out of the corner of his eye and decided to follow it, being aware that it had been unwell for the last couple of weeks. Although he searched, he could not see it anywhere. The next day he mentioned this to the gardener, explaining how he was glad to see the cat had recovered from its illness. The gardener thanked him for his kind words but then explained to Mr Cooke that his cat had been knocked down by a car in front of the hall the day before. It was killed immediately. Was it the ghost of the gardener's cat that Mr Cooke had seen? Had he just been making his way home, to the wander the house he knew so well?

A pair of ghostly duellists from the Civil War period are also said to haunt the great hall. One afternoon a guest was reading in the great chamber when the two men bustled into the room. Annoyed at being disturbed she shouted to them to stop immediately and to go outside; they both ignored her and carried on with their duel. When the woman realised she was being ignored, she pulled the rope to summon one of the servants but no one arrived. She returned to her chair but the duel continued in front of her. Suddenly, one of the men was slashed across the arm and started to bleed heavily. They then left the room.

A couple of hours later the woman told her host of the trouble she had encountered while trying to read in the hall, and asked him if he could ask them to refrain from duelling inside. He was most confused, particularly when the guest mentioned that one gentleman had sustained an injury. She took her host to see the blood marks on one of the rugs in the hall, but when they looked closer there were no bloodstains to be seen.

An apparition of a black priest is also seen at Athelhampton, usually in daylight hours. One of the housemaids in the 1960s was said to be doing her usual duties when she heard footsteps behind her. She turned to see the distinct figure of a hooded gentleman, dressed in black, and standing outside one of the doors. It is believed that this is the spirit of the kindly Catholic priest who lived with the Martyn family. He is still seen and heard to this day, but his presence is not alarming as he seems curious to watch what is going on around the house, particularly when members of the public are visiting.

A grey lady is said to be the most common spirit sighted at the hall and has been seen by many of its owners over the years. Mr Robert Cooke admits to seeing the woman in the early hours of the morning as she appeared to pass through the walls of the east wing to the yellow bedroom. Until recently, one of the rooms in the house had a small wooden crib on display; however, the current owner removed it as it rocked by itself. Was the grey lady rocking the crib? She has also been witnessed by some of the staff. One evening, a housemaid noticed a woman sitting in a chair in one of the rooms. Thinking she was a member of the public, the maid approached to mention the house was now closed to visitors. However, the figure rose from the chair and walked through the wooden panelling. The keeper in the 1980s also witnessed the apparition and described her as, 'wearing a rather full, plain dress and a gauzy sort of head-dress, then she gradually faded away in front of me.'

Whether you believe these accounts or not, Athelhampton has become a centre for paranormal enthusiasts. As it is still a private home it is understandable that groups are not allowed to stay overnight, but many visit during the day

A visit to Athelhampton is recommended whether you are interested in the paranormal or not – you can be sure of a warm welcome from Patrick, Andrea, all their staff and possibly from all their ghosts too!

The Maiden at Mai Dun

Maiden Castle is the largest Iron Age hill fort in Europe and covers an area of 47 acres. 'Maiden' derives from the Celtic 'Mai Dun' which means 'great hill'. It is situated just 2 miles south of Dorchester in Dorset. It is truly an amazing place: even after more than 2000 years, the earthworks are immense, some ramparts rising to a height of 6 metres (20 feet). It is thought that the construction of Maiden Castle began around 3000 BC and flint tools and other object dating from that time have been found. The late Stone Age/ early Bronze Age people who lived there built a massive ditch and bank some 545 metres in length. There are Bronze Age burial mounds on the right hand end of the Castle. The present hill fort as we see it today, was started during the Iron Age around 450 - 300 BC when the area of the fort was extended and the ramparts and ditches were enlarged. Three ditches were dug, the earth removed being used to build the ramparts. A wooden fence would have been built along the ramparts with wooden gates at the entrances. The entrances were not aligned therefore making it more difficult for opposing forces to gain entry. At the time of the Roman invasion in 43 AD, Maiden Castle was inhabited by the Durotriges tribe. The battle to take the castle was a bloody one: the Romans under Vespasian finally victorious. Recent excavations have uncovered the bodies of 38 Iron Age warriors, buried with food and drink for their journey into the after life. A Roman temple was built at Maiden Castle in the 4th century, the foundations of which can still be seen today. The fort was abandoned shortly after this time, although it may have been occupied during early Saxon times. It has certainly been deserted for the last 1400 years or so.

Extract taken from www.historic-uk.com

To reach the top of the fort, there is a short dirt track where some visitors have seen more than they bargained for. On the approach to the fort's main entrance, at the end of the track, there have been sightings of a beautiful, young woman dressed in white, with long, dark hair, who

Aerial view of Maiden Castle.

The track-road entrance to Maiden Castle, where the spirit of a girl still runs scared.

A burial mound less than 100ft away from Maiden Castle.

scampers about barefoot. She is said to look scared and as though she is looking for someone, as though invisible forces are following her. Those who have tried to follow the distraught maiden before she disappears have tried to interact with her; however, it appears that she may not just be a spectral recording of an event gone because she has been reported at different parts of the fort at different times of the day. She is only ever seen in the summer giving rise to speculation that she was perhaps a sacrificial virgin and made an escape. Is this why she is always seen running and looking around? Sadly it appears she is destined to stay at the fort trying to escape her fate.

Poor Betsey Caine

Dewlish is a small village lying to the north-east of Dorchester. It stands close to the ominous Devils Brook but it is not the Lord of Darkness who haunts this village.

Betsey Caine was a local farm girl who, in 1830, hanged herself after her love affair with a local boy went sadly wrong. Suicide in those days was frowned on by the church and so she was not allowed a burial in the churchyard. She was buried in woodland on her father's farmland and the funeral was a quiet, family affair in the middle of the night, because of the shame her suicide brought on her family and the village as a whole. Not long after the burial, villagers started seeing the ghost of Betsey around the village. One gentleman, who had been away when she died and consequently had not heard of her passing, apparently had a long conversation with her ghost whilst she was sitting on a gate leading into the woodland where she had been buried. When he returned to his family he mentioned his conversation with young Betsey and he learned that he had been conversing with the ghost of a girl who had been dead for over two weeks.

Sightings of Betsey steadily increased over the weeks and it was said that her soul was not truly at rest – as a religious girl, she had not had a church burial. Soon, villagers started to avoid the gate which led to the woods after dark, but as it was a path to near by Milborne St Andrew, this was sometimes not possible. The path has since become a road and it is said that on a certain stretch, on a sweeping bend, the ghost of poor Betsey Caine can still be seen in the headlights of passing motorists. Perhaps she will continue to haunt the area until her bones are removed from their shallow grave and moved to the churchyard. The sad truth is though, now

The Old Rectory at Maiden Newton.

the road has been built, it may be impossible to know where she was buried, meaning that this unfortunate girl could be wandering this quiet country lane for the foreseeable future.

The Ghosts of Maiden Newton

> Maiden Newton is a village situated on the A356 north of Dorchester and straddles the River Frome. During excavations in the eighteenth century, a pavement dating to the Romano-British period was found in the village. The Domesday Book states the village had two watermills. By the fifteenth century, Maiden Newton had become a market town. Houses in the village range in dates from modern properties mixed successfully with old fifteenth century stone constructions. The parish church, St Mary's is mainly Norman and Medieval however a blocked off Saxon doorway is still evident and it is said that this is one of the oldest in the country.
>
> Extract taken from www.dorsets.co.uk

Despite the long history of the church, the ghost who is said to roam the churchyard is more recent, and was first seen by a gentleman walking his

St Mary's Church at Maiden Newton may be haunted by the spirit of a musketeer.

dog over forty years ago. As the man approached the side of the church he almost bumped into a man walking towards him. He was dressed strangely, wearing an almost flat, velvet-looking cap and a matching outfit with a gold-coloured sash. In fact he looked like a musketeer and did not acknowledge the gentleman and carried walking down the side of the church. The gentleman, thinking he had stumbled on a re-enactment, glanced over his shoulder but the figure was nowhere to be seen. Speculation in the village suggests that the spectre was a musketeer and damage to St Mary's Church by musket fire during the English Civil War seems to support this theory.

Maiden Newton Station is still considered to be the heart of the Wessex Line and used to have a branch line to Bridport. The track is now disused and forms part of a nature walk through the water meadows, where the phantom of an old gentleman with a coal-stained face is said to appear from nowhere, disappearing as quickly as he arrived. Was he a railway worker from former times?

Dancing Ladies

Herrison Hall in Charlton Down was the former ballroom of a large psychiatric hospital. The old buildings have been partly converted and the old ballroom is now the village hall.

The faint outlines of two women dressed in white have been seen gliding around the floor of the hall, giggling to themselves as they go. They pose no threat to anyone and the few people that have seen them remember them with fondness despite the fact that they may indeed be former residents of the hospital. This goes to prove that while it is all very exciting thinking about gruesome ghosts at an old mental hospital, the reality is that if the hospital was a good hospital like this one, then they appear to pose no more harm to us than the average ghost!

A Truly Spoken Dorset Poem

> William Barnes was born in 1801 at Bagber, near Sturminster Newton in North Dorset. He was educated locally and worked as a solicitor's clerk until 1823, when he became a schoolmaster. In 1827 he married Julia Miles. Her death, in 1852, affected him deeply; many of his poems describe his love for her. He was ordained in 1848 and was appointed curate at Whitcombe near Dorchester. Barnes died in 1886; his obituary in the Saturday Review read: 'There is no doubt that he is the best pastoral poet we possess, the most sincere, the most genuine, the most theocritan; and that the dialect is but a very thin veil hiding from us some of the most delicate and finished verse written in our time.
>
> Extract taken from www.people.bath.ac.uk

Barnes was dedicated to his home and also to the county town of Dorchester where he had done much of his training. His spirit is said to reside now in Bagber and his poem *The Young that Died in Beauty* can apparently still be heard, being recited by Barnes himself when the wind blows through the trees in the village as he continues to mourn the death of his wife:

The William Barnes statue outside St Peter's Church, showing his attachment to Dorchester.

An' yeet the church, where prayer do rise
Vrom thoughtvul souls, wi' downcast eyes,
An' village greens, a – beat half beare
By dancers that do meet, an' wear
Such merry looks at feast an' feair,
Do gather under leatest skies,
Their bloomen cheaks an' sparklen eyes,
Though young ha' died in beauty.

But still the dead shall mwore than Keep
The beauty ov their early sleep;
Where comely looks shall never wear
Uncomely, under tweil an' ceare.
The feair at death be always feair,
Still feair to livers' thought an' love,
An' feairer still to God above,
Than when they died in beauty.

Other local titles published by The History Press

Haunted Poole
JULIE HARWOOD

From heart-stopping accounts of apparitions and manifestations to first-hand encounters with ghouls and spirits, this collection of stories contains new and well-known spooky tales from in and around Poole.

Drawing on historical and contemporary sources, *Haunted Poole* contains a chilling range of ghostly phenonema, including the town's own tragic Romeo and Juliet tale, legendary Poole pirate Harry Paye and his ghostly galleon, the screams of Alice Beard and ghoulish beggars wandering the streets.

978 0 7524 4503 8

Haunted Cornwall
PAUL NEWMAN

For anyone who would like to know why Cornwall is called the most haunted place in Britain, this collection of stories of apparitions, manifestations and related supernatural incidents from around the Duchy provides the answer. The book features a gory medieval murder at Poundstock; a gruelling exorcism at Botathan; the spectre of Annie George at the First and Last Inn at Sennen; a 'human double' clocking in for work at St Austell and a phantom stagecoach on the Mevagissey road.

978 0 7524 3668 5

Haunted Brighton
ALAN MURDIE

From spine-chilling accounts of apparitions, spirits and other supernatural visitors to first-hand encounters with polite ghosts, malign presences and poltergeists, this collection of stories contains both well-known and hitherto unpublished cases of hauntings from in and around Brighton.

Drawing on historical, scientific and contemporary sources, *Haunted Brighton* contains a chilling range of ghostly phenomena, from the ghost of Cary Grant at the Rottingdean Club to the Screaming Skull in the Lanes and the ghost who spelt out 'prove me innocent!' at Preston Manor.

978 0 7524 3829 0

Haunted Winchester
MATTHEW FELDWICK

From accounts of apparitions and related supernatural phenomena to first-hand encounters with ghouls and spirits, this collection of stories contains new and well-known spooky tales from around the ancient city of Winchester.

This selection includes tales of spectral monks at Winchester Cathedral and phantom horses in the Cathedral Close, as well as stories of the Eclipse Inn where Dame Alice Lisle, condemned by Judge Jefferies, still walks, and the sounds of spectral digging in one of the many tunnels which once riddled the city. This phenomenal gathering of ghostly goings-on will captivate anyone interested in the supernatural history of the area.

978 0 7524 3846 7

If you are interested in purchasing other books published by The History Press, or in case you have difficulty finding any History Press books in your local bookshop, you can also place orders directly through our website

www.thehistorypress.co.uk